T0113300

Oxycontin or Oxytocin:

Addiction, Recovery, Prevention

Sue Berry McMurray

authorHOUSE®

AuthorHouse™
1663 Liberty Drive
Bloomington, IN 47403
www.authorhouse.com
Phone: 1 (800) 839-8640

© *2016 Sue Berry McMurray. All rights reserved.*

No part of this book may be reproduced, stored in a retrieval system, or
transmitted by any means without the written permission of the author.

Published by AuthorHouse 10/12/2016

ISBN: 978-1-5246-4517-5 (sc)
ISBN: 978-1-5246-4516-8 (e)

Print information available on the last page.

Any people depicted in stock imagery provided by Thinkstock are models,
and such images are being used for illustrative purposes only.
Certain stock imagery © Thinkstock.

This book is printed on acid-free paper.

Because of the dynamic nature of the Internet, any web addresses or links contained in
this book may have changed since publication and may no longer be valid. The views
expressed in this work are solely those of the author and do not necessarily reflect the
views of the publisher, and the publisher hereby disclaims any responsibility for them.

CONTENTS

DISCLAIMER

In keeping with the emphasis on anonymity in the 12 Step programs, all original names have been changed and any identifying descriptions have been removed.

Chapter

What Exactly Is Addiction?

For the purposes of this book, addiction can be described as the habitual pattern of seeking and needing substances or behaviors plus clinging to false beliefs…in order to relieve painful unconscious states, with an underlying denial and inability to pause and recognize any disturbing results from this way of living.

This enlarges our list of addictions, and allows us to see many more ways we get 'stuck', while realizing the insidious role of denial and its origins which can even allow pain to be passed from one generation to another unknowingly.

In everyday terms, an addiction is something you do over and over again, expecting different results, until (hopefully) you realize it is ruining your life and your relationships. We 'thought' we just wanted to get high, not 'forget' our past!

Addiction occurs when our brains are frozen in a certain pattern which we are unable to recognize, losing the flexibility of choice in the matter even though our rational side may try to stop but finds itself unable to resist. It takes a much deeper assessment of ourselves, and much more powerful tools of healing than 'just say no'.

The classic case, of course, since man first pressed grapes, is the alcoholic.

And in America around 1935, it was alcoholics, out of desperation and the sentence of death, who developed a set of steps which has given us, around the globe, help in breaking addiction. Neuroscience has followed, giving us more clues to what goes on. Increasing knowledge about how human beings develop in the very early stages of life has shed light on the denial which is the twin of most addictions.

We now see the full array of addictions. Drug use has proliferated, and drug addiction has increased, despite the 'war' waged against it. Eating disorders abound, highlighted by celebrities such as Princess Diana, whose bulimia was made public.

Gambling can become an addiction, with its heightened reward anticipation. Sexual addiction and pornography certainly make the list, prompting a cover issue of Time magazine recently.

But just as debilitating, addiction to rage has brought about therapy groups which are commonly termed 'anger management'. Many drivers exhibit this addiction when underlying cracks in their psychological makeup reveal a desire to run people off the road, or 'cut them off".

Of course, workaholics work. And in so doing, they fill every moment they can, leaving as little time as possible to look at the failing marriage, or the out-of-control children. Work covers up the pain of actually seeing reality.

One of the most insidious addictions is a constantly controlling and caretaking behavior with others, in an attempt to dodge one's own deep emotional pain.

The list goes on and on, and the spell can only be broken by some method of slowly unlocking the blind denial that seals it shut so tightly. This is a tall order.

The face and details of addiction are many.

The man or woman who is red-faced and bleary-eyed, with an unmistakable slightly sour smell, refusing to recognize the slide into uncontrolled use of alcohol.

The teenager whose eyes are dilated constantly, skipping school, breaking and entering, lying to teachers, parents, and police officers.

The hovering 'addict' who is constantly caretaking, and oblivious to these behaviors while taking over situations and controlling others in matters large and small, with no time to sense or own personal pain.

My aunt had a friend who died, ostensibly of a 'heart attack'. When I spoke to her daughter, she confided that the physician had found her mother's liver 'something from the bowery'. A bottle of vodka was found in the tank of her toilet!

But these secret sins can be recognized and addressed by various means.

This book will look at them through the 12Step lens.

Recently I heard a man share with great anguish in a meeting. He told very movingly about an incident that very week. While his wife was sleeping, he managed to find her purse, locate her wallet, and unzip the bill section. His hand was on a twenty, as it had been so many times in the past, to buy his alcohol.

Suddenly he was able to pause, as he had NOT been able to do in the past. He returned the bill, returned the wallet, and returned the purse to the drawer.

The next day, he told his wife what he had done.

She put her face in her hands, and cried. For joy.

So, these addictive patterns can be changed, but not that easily.

Denial can be extremely strong, resisting a breakthrough for many reasons.

But when it crumbles, the person can then begin to be set free.

Because the 12 Step programs are completely without cost, totally non-discriminatory, and available everywhere from here to Beijing and back, I will try to base some of my observations on the tools they offer.

Any mention of members in the meetings will adhere to the basic rule of anonymity, with any identifying elements removed, except in the case of Patrick Kennedy, who in his book, A Common Struggle, courageously outs himself.

One clue to the premise of this book is found on page 79 of The 12 Steps and 12 Traditions in our literature:

'Very deep, sometimes quite forgotten, damaging conflicts persist below the level of consciousness. At the time of these occurrences, they may actually have given our emotions violent twists which have since discolored our personalities and altered our lives for the worst'.

The 12 Step fellowships start the recovery ball rolling.

The middle steps help us uncover these violent twists to our personalities, and most importantly, give us specific, concrete, and simple tools to use, if we so choose.

Another very important quote from the Big Book (Alcoholics Anonymous) on page 152:

'I know I must get along without liquor, but how can I?

Have you a sufficient substitute?

Yes, there is a substitute and it is vastly more than that.

It is a fellowship in Alcoholics Anonymous.'

Notes or Thoughts

Chapter

What Methods Have Been Used Against Denial and Addiction?

In the past, we have declared a 'war' on drug addiction, and continued to endorse the mindset that says addicts and alcoholics are weak-willed persons with moral failings so great that punishment, shame, and incarceration must be called in against them. Ostracism and guilt were used in an attempt to 'bring them around'.

The enormous stigma toward people with addictions was thought to be a crucial factor in helping them to turn their lives around. Punish their sins!

In reading Chasing the Scream: The First and Last Days of the War on Drugs, by Johann Hari, I learned that early on, at the end of Prohibition, the organization to fight liquor was simply refitted to fight drugs, thus ensuring job continuation.

Nancy Reagan's simplistic urging to say 'no' was advice from the non-addicted to the addict, with no serious investigation of what motivated people to drink and drug.

In fact, like the children who act out in school and are repeated called 'bad', labels embedded the idea that addicts were fatally flawed in their very being, resulting in more 'bad' behavior.

Now however, if you google the war on drugs, you will find a clip of Sixty Minutes featuring a new and different approach.

I am reminded of the time I was sent out by NC Health and Human Services to do workshops on behavior management in preschools. One school used shame, guilt, and name-calling to rein in 'bad behavior', but wondered why the youngsters were so sullen, angry, and hateful afterwards.

How can we change our attitudes towards alcoholics and addicts without condoning their behavior? What clues can we get from basic 12 Step practices and beliefs?

First of all, the 12 Step programs say to their members, 'We are not bad, getting good, but sick, getting better'. Alcoholism and addiction are seen as a chronic disease, for lack of a better word, never to be absolutely cured, but instead held at bay while a new and different life is created by following the 12Steps and connecting to the people in the fellowship.

Acceptance and inclusion is a hallmark of most 12Step fellowships, infusing the meetings with tolerance and care for each and every member, despite the great disparity in age, race, education, social position and IQ usually found there.

There are no rules and record-keeping, except the basic caveat to keep the meeting civil in order to serve both the old timers and the newcomers as they seek recovery.

There is no group or committee who can punish or shame a member.

The meetings are open for all members to use for as much growth as they wish, at a pace they feel is comfortable.

Speaker meetings feature someone 'telling their story', outlining personally 'what it was like, what happened, and how it is now'. Discussion meetings allow members to share on a step or a topic, from their experience. Literature meetings have a format that allows round-robin reading in the Big Book or some other approved literature.

Closed meetings are for addicts or alcoholics exclusively. Open meetings allow visitors, sometimes the students who are training in the field of addiction.

All this, in my opinion, helps to break through the impenetrable wall of denial which goes hand in hand with common characteristics of any person suffering from alcoholism or addiction of any kind. Our minds remain tightly closed.

Denial is not a river in Egypt, says one 12Step slogan. But why that denial exists is something we must try to understand and penetrate. Where does denial originate?

That is one main key to the recovery and prevention of addiction. Child development and neuroscience offer us some hard- to- understand clues which help to see and explore more about recovery and prevention.

What could possibly be the origin of a continuation to repeatedly drink or drug with no regard at all for consequences? 'I am hurting no one', we vow emphatically.

My years of therapy and research finally revealed possible answers to this baffling question although I was doubtful for a long time.

How could anyone be so oblivious to the evidences of addiction, denying the power of substances and behaviors? 'Who, ME?' we ask incredulously.

What in the world was so strong and powerful that it could slam shut the doors of reason and render a person unable to see the truth? Why this blindness?

After a few courses in human development I began to see some light. Emotional pain, and shame about that pain often closed down any ability to recognize and own up to the growing signs of destructive addiction.

Notes or Thoughts

Chapter

Implicit and Explicit Memory

The first inkling I had about memory came about in a heated argument one day with my therapist.

I was absolutely certain that memory was a clear unequivocal straight line, and more importantly, that I had CONTROL and KNOWLEDGE of it.

And I was not about to even try to consider that there were powerful memories and feelings and attitudes that were operating without my knowledge or direction.

This was just too frightening.

With angry words, I assured him he was wrong, dead wrong.

Little did I know how important his information would be in understanding the absolute choke hold of denial.

The brain is not just for learning math and doing well in school

The brain is an organ equipped to help us survive and thrive against all odds, and denial seems to be part of its wondrous plan in this undertaking if we can only put aside our strenuous doubts and look more closely, with an openness that may allow us to change our minds, and permit that 'aha' moment. Just as we 'pass out' from physical pain, we can become unconscious of emotional pain.

We do not need to be familiar with the Yakovlevian torque between the two hemispheres of the brain. We only need to see how the brain serves our survival.

We simply need to observe how very strong denial can be in our own lives and the lives of others when it serves basic survival.

Addiction is one thing, but the denial which locks it in is another.

Understanding some things about denial can help us in recovery from addiction and also unlock some new avenues in prevention.

So, let's begin with a look at the whole sweep of human development.

What I learned and now know, is that the deepest, most important learning we do is not in grade school.

The central and most basic life-giving lessons each individual learns are those that occur from conception on until the person leaves the family to make it alone.

And the part I had difficulty with was that these lessons are most often stored away in unconscious memory. They live on beneath the surface of awareness.

We are not really conscious of them.

This was a concept I had a tremendously hard time accepting.

Until finally I understood, at long last, the truth of it, and resistance BROKE.

What opened my eyes was reading The Handbook of Attachment, edited by Cassidy and Shaver.

I found out that studies and research showed that each infant developed its way of being to an amazing extent from how it was embedded in the maternal relationship and in the family constellation. We shape ourselves by our attachment environment.

The child had no choice in the matter at all, being totally dependent on its caretakers and their unique ways of being. We take the place others create for us to take.

For instance, if the mother suffered from severe depression, the baby learned to live with, and be marked by, that depression.

If the mother was violent, the child developed a knowledge of, and reaction to, violence.

If the caretaker noted the youngster's needs for food, warmth, and comfort, and met those needs well enough, the little person grew up comfortable with those feelings.

But what was impossible for me to grasp at first was that all this learning was implicit. It remains underground, calcifying its hold.

Unconscious learning was taking place.

This learning was so deeply buried inside the individual that there was no awareness except for the Freudian slip or the occasional cryptic clue.

An entire structure inside the person was created by the shape of their family system, unbeknownst to his or her explicit consciousness.

And when leaving the nest, a young man or woman carried within them a powerful blueprint for actions, attitudes, emotions, and beliefs of which they were unaware.

It was as if there were a sign pinned to the back of shirt or dress, describing what shape they had been molded into, which only others could read.

Oldest child, responsible for five younger siblings when Mom was drunk.

Little boy, watching father beat mother, and unable to intervene.

Two young girls, molested by an uncle.

Youngster left alone in a hospital for long months of treatment.

Seven year old, manipulated for affection by divorced parents.

The list goes on and on.

And because the learning has taken place implicitly, the person, now grown up, has no earthly idea that he or she can change, because there is no way to see and begin to understand the structure he constantly lives in. Often, this is when addiction begins to come on the scene. An unknown, skewed structure creates great pain!

Notes or Thoughts

Chapter

Removing The
Wall of Denial

I t is my firm belief that the strength of the wall of denial is very closely correlated with the degree of emotional pain in one's implicit, unconscious bodily memories which are stored unknowingly from the beginning.

This is not a cop-out, or a call to self-pity and excuses.

This is not some wild idea to take people 'off the hook'.

This is not an unsupported opinion flying in the face of good sense.

This seems to be a basic fact very pertinent to addiction and its recovery and prevention. This fact can be part of the key that unlocks addiction.

Why do some recover from alcohol and drugs and some do not? We all are familiar with persons who have died, unrecovered, from continued addiction

Is this simply because they were too bad, too evil, too no-count?

Maybe so. That is certainly what we have been led to believe.

But bear with me, and try to leave the door open for another look, a deeper look, at addiction, which may give us clues to help in recovery and prevention.

Before we beef up the war on drugs, let's investigate some additional paths to explore, which may shed new light on this frightening and baffling subject.

First of all, we have NO idea what any person we meet has stored in implicit childhood memory of which they are not aware. We cannot really judge.

On the surface, a physician may appear content with her profession, while deep inside there is the unspoken and unexamined fact that her father needed her to replace the son in medical school who was killed in an automobile accident. From an early age, these kids were used by dad to complete his own dreams.

What about the young girl, overpowered by an intoxicated uncle, and told never to tell, who sought out drugs and alcohol to numb the emotional pain of silence.

What about the soldier dealing with the anguish of shooting civilians, echoing a lifelong tendency to 'explode' following a disturbing childhood lived in the battleground of domestic violence.

In the neuropsychological words of British physician Iain McGilchrist, from his book The Master and His Emissary: The Divided Brain and the Making of the Western World: 'The sense of self emerges from the activity of the brain in interaction with other selves'.

I am not saying that every single addict walks with denied emotional pain.

But yes, I am saying that, upon deeper investigation, a great many do.

What keeps the addict from recognizing both the connection of his addiction to consequences and the reality of his emotional pain?

Denial.

And why is it that some break through this denial and others do not?

There are certainly many reasons for this.

But I sincerely believe that the depth, intensity, and prolongation of emotional pain, plus the lack of enough early, positive attachment experiences are a huge but unrecognized factor in both failure to achieve sobriety and in repeated relapses.

If this is true it would have a profound on the treatment and prevention of addiction.

Reading In the Realm of Hungry Ghosts by Gabor Mate' opens our eyes to the wisdom of looking at addicts a different way.

Mate' introduces us to a section in Vancouver, Canada where his work in the field of addiction includes severe, debilitated, and 'crazy' clients who cannot stop using.

His dedication to this population comes from his own experience as a Jewish baby who lost large parts of both extended families in the Holocaust and had to be hidden to escape death himself in the final days before the war ended.

His mother would play music to calm herself, and Mate' sees his sometimes compulsive overbuying of CD's when stressed, as a consequence. He recounts once suddenly turning over a difficult obstetrical delivery to his fellow physician and running to the shop to purchase as many musical recordings as possible, some of which he confessed he never even played.

His accounts of difficult and very trying addicts reveal his care and compassion, along with anger when they relapse and try to 'play' him.

We meet, in photo and narrative, many of those addicts which he treats, and we too are by turns both compassionate and then angry.

It is the same anger and compassion we feel in a 12Step meeting upon hearing that someone has 'gone back out'.

Helplessness and fear.

But reading Mate's book can turn the feeling of condemnation to one of more kindness and understanding as we come to see where these folks have come from.

Our hopes are lifted as one individual seems to break through, only to be dashed as another descent into hell takes place. Mate' is relentless in his care and concern.

Clean needles are provided, and even when death by overdose is imminent, love and support are provided, giving some sort of attachment at life's end.

Notes or Thoughts

Chapter

5

Addiction and Attachment

If we look closely at addiction, we see an alarming attachment to alcohol, drugs, or destructive behaviors which literally has taken control of the individual, becoming more and more a way of life, closing off free and flexible growth and change.

In a way, this could be seen as a 'sealing off' from oneself, due to painful attachment configurations which came about in infancy and childhood.

In talking to various members of 12 Step programs, I have found a wide variety and intensity of difficult attachments experienced while growing up.

One young woman was kidnapped by her white father from her Native American mother, and thereafter lived under the care of her step-mother who berated her constantly.

Another young woman grew up in a family where dad had also impregnated mom's sister, who lived next door with her baby.

One wonderful woman I knew had a child, at twelve, by her own father. The information on the birth certificate was changed and the child became 'sister'.

Several of the guys had grown up in an alcoholic home and had seen father beat mother repeatedly but knew they were incapable of overpowering him, so stood by helplessly. Some became domestic abusers.

One man was beaten so mercilessly and often by his mother that the emotional scars were still there at 80.

Another fellow, brought up in poverty and alcoholism, was rented out as a boy for sex with any man who would pay for it.

These are cases which stand out, but others also involve children who had to come up with a distorted attachment pattern.

Often, children with a severely ill sibling over long years may turn out with emotional marks of distress from lack of attention and closeness with parents.

One of the most illuminating books I have read is Ghosts from the Nursery by Robin Karr-Morse. It deals with trauma that infants experience, during a time period that we have long believed is impervious to 'memories'. Babies don't remember!

And it would seem that the young do 'forget', except that now we are learning that Nature seals over these wounds until later, so that the child can attach the best it can during the years of dependency to whatever the family system offers.

Consequently, we look superficially at a person and never dream that there may be subterranean wounds that we are not aware of at all.

In good enough therapy, these treacherous faults may be discovered and mended. And in the 12Step programs, members work together to unearth and de-toxify old twisted patterns of attachment which underlie their turbulent lives of addiction.

But it seems to take two things. One is being able to finally look squarely at the trail of destruction, chaos and depression we have created daily...'hitting bottom'. And the other thing is some unseen bit of slowly developing trust that, with following suggestions, things very gradually will get better, the more you can practice attachment and work the steps. People sharing in the meetings are the proof.

But here is the catch.

With strong habits of poor attachment already deep in our psyche, we are deathly afraid of any new calls to attachment, except to alcohol, drugs, depression, low self-esteem, isolation, control and caretaking, repeated sexual stimulation, accumulating more and more wealth, eating, pain meds...the list goes on and on. These activities numb the emotional anguish we feel from painful attachment, blotting it out. And we tend to deny any problems, as long as we can get our 'fix'.

Of course, one of the most crucial events that might underlie emotional pain is birth.

The infant is delivered into this world and not much is recorded about the details.

A beautiful account of birth into water (Birth Without Violence by Frederick Leboyer) gives us photographs of a peaceful baby having entered this world, smiling.

But at times there are events during birth which can live on unconsciously, played out in mysterious ways.

We see this in the case of Rosemary, the one Kennedy sibling of the original nine, who suffered some mental confusion.

One account revealed that the delivery doctor was detained, and the nurse in attendance at the Kennedy home held the baby girl back until finally he arrived on the scene, resulting in a short period of oxygen deprivation.

The point I am trying to make, once again, is that many things can happen, and be forgotten, in the early parts of anyone's life journey, buried by the focus on adulthood. Buried by the sure belief that babies don't register emotional pain.

It is extremely easy to say to ourselves 'children forget'. It is a human tendency to regard the young as Teflon beings who immediately shed traumatic experiences.

But we see now that this is not so, even though it is difficult to understand.

My wakeup call was an incident where a bus full of small school children was buried under a hillside of earth for a fairly long stretch of time. At rescue, they were not hurried to 'just forget about it', but instead, encouraged to talk about their feelings for some weeks with counselors who knew that denying feelings makes one ill.

Notes or Thoughts

Chapter

Changing Old Feelings

Neuroscience has discovered the power of these old states of mind to continue to live on in our very cells, refusing to surface, as we unconsciously live out their unrecognized negative behaviors and beliefs in our everyday lives while being helpless to change.

A Canadian neurofeedback center located in British Columbia is attempting to bring about psychospiritual transformation through the use of alpha brainwave training.

Dr. James Hardt is director of this center, calling it The Biocybernaut Institute.

Hardt found that many of the Biocybernaut participants were experiencing great difficulty when they encountered formerly repressed psychological feelings which surfaced during the work.

However, their scores increased significantly when helped to exercise any sort of attempt at forgiveness. Forgiving others, but also forgiving oneself.

The presence of forgiveness seemed critical to the release of emotional trauma that may have accumulated through years of painful interactions with one's environment due to personal, familial, cultural, or other forms of conflict.

At first blush we dig in our heels and regard this as a joke.

I am reminded of the New Yorker cartoon of a business man talking on the phone in his office to his boss.

This is how the caption read:

'I am sorry my report was late…I did not get enough holding from my mother as a baby'.

We have always tended somehow to feel that this way of thinking is ridiculous.

Reading the account of these findings at The Biocybernaut Institute in a recently published book, *Principles of Practical Psychology* by Erik Linderman, I was rocked back again from my disbelief. EEG brainwaves do not lie.

The reason I know this is because I did some work a few years back with Dr. Dan Chartier in Raleigh NC.

Dr. Chartier is a very respected practitioner in neurofeedback.

He first took a 'map' of my brainwaves, explaining to me the different frequencies such as Alpha, Beta, Theta, and Gamma.

At a subsequent session, he hooked me up to a computer and I was instructed to listen for a faint train whistle which indicated that I had reached calmness. (I suffer from PTSD). Since I would tend to drift back off into an anxious state, I had to learn to practice breathing slowly and deeply, bringing myself back again eventually to the train whistle and my calmer state.

There were much more sophisticated applications, but due to the expense, I was unable to continue this treatment although I could see that it had great merit.

However, I also grew to understand that the 12Step programs offered a similar calming effect in their simple hour-long meetings where folks gathered together and shared their progress and growth. Something was going on in those rooms.

The diversity in these meetings add a profound sense of strength and unity, and of course, they were entirely free, although a basket was passed for contributions.

From many different directions, I was learning some basic facts which made sense.

I began to see that addiction seemed to progress out of a deep seated feeling of malaise, coupled with a terrible need to numb oneself out and not feel anything.

Of course non-addicted people naturally judge things from their own viewpoint and experience, and offer genuinely honest advice to follow their example and just put the drink or drug down. They are able to do this, and believe others can also.

'Others' simply are unable to just stop because unconsciously buried emotional pain is often too huge and too frightening to look at. So we continue to seek numbness. However, the practices suggested by the 12Step programs can heal, and do, with growing numbers all over the world. Why?

First of all, they offer a new attachment.

Members describe the fellowship as a 'we' program, and indeed, all twelve steps state or imply the pronoun WE. Togetherness is fostered in as many ways as possible, and to the extent the newcomers can gradually feel they are a part of the group, recovery from addiction slowly occurs.

Working the steps with a sponsor, aided by hearing in meetings personal sharing about growth and change and challenge from other members, pulls the individual painfully but surely out of the isolation of addiction.

Joining a home group gives the new person a feeling of belonging, attachment if you will, and also a list of first names and telephone numbers to call.

At first, this is hard.

The phrase 'pick up that five hundred pound telephone' expresses the difficulty of engaging in attachment when we have known emotional pain with communication in our past. Many deep-seated fears hold us in paralyzing thrall.

But at some point, the pain and destruction of drinking and drugging that we are now able to SEE drives us to overcome our fears, and we make that phone call.

Notes or Thoughts

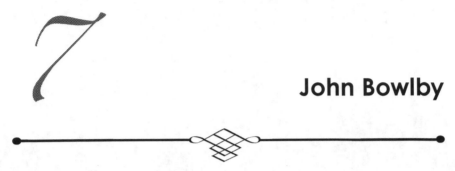

Chapter

7

John Bowlby

M any of the discoveries about attachment stem from one man and his colleagues. John Bowlby first noticed the fact from ethology that a gosling would attach itself to any moving, living creature if the true parent were not available. Connection!

We know that mammals are social creatures, needing contact and connection above all else. In The Archaeology of Mind: Neuroevolutionary Origins of Human Emotions by Jaak Panksepp, we find a detailed account of how our limbic brains evolved, giving us communication through emotions and body language to make up for lack of superior size and strength in the life or death struggle for survival long ago. Mammals strongly cling to each other. Hachito, the Akita dog, waited for his master at a Japanese subway for nine years, not knowing he had died.

Bowlby and his students even identified specific patterns of attachment by a simple experiment: toddlers were separated for a short period from their mothers, minded by a stranger, and then returned to Mom. The target information was the behavior and attitude of the child at the time of reunion.

Secure attachment was evidenced perhaps by giving Mom a smile or a physical hug, for instance, after which the youngster took up play again, regaining the ongoing bedrock security felt in his or her basic individual life attachment situation.

The really disturbing results came about, however, when the little one displayed discomfort upon return to the mother, revealing clues that the learned relationship of attachment was either uncomfortable, or worse, very emotionally painful.

Bowlby's trainees later found that the attahment profile continued to be the same, secure, insecure, or disorganized, as the individual matured, and it even predicted similar marriage attachments which would later be sought out for familiarity.

Let me give one example from a person I have known well in a 12Step setting which might shed some light on attachment and the tenacity and power of attachment beliefs and positions.

Let's call my friend Ed.

At birth, Ed presented as a baby boy and was welcomed as such by his traditional parents who were delighted to have a son, and were determined to help and encourage him in sports and other manly pursuits.

However, Ed found their vision for him very uncomfortable.

The pattern of attachment thus grew tense as Ed gravitated toward other non-macho interests, and his parents grew alarmed at this and doubled down on baseball, hockey, and tennis.

Being dependent on his parents, Ed did his best to please them, but he felt a great and growing unease in the jock world, creating an unconsciously untenable pattern of emotionally painful attachment. He did what they wanted, but he lost himself.

In high school and college he went out for sports, but what seemed to be okay on the surface simply hid his deep underlying reluctance. Drinking and drugging numbed the mounting emotional pain he lived with, and increased the denial he had that anything was amiss.

While others eventually gave up experimental drugs, Ed continued, and then slowly increased his use. He graduated from pharmacy school, and began to steal pain meds while on his first job. He was busted, but was convinced he could stop. But he couldn't. Denial had sealed shut any doorway of insight into his situation.

The old pattern he had developed for attachment continued as he became more ambivalent about his sexual orientation but could not reconcile that with the conservative, extremely religious fears of his parents about homosexuality.

Ed tried the 12 Step programs, but his fears and isolation and despair won out.

He could not engage in recovery, and he ended it all with a gun in his mouth.

The story of Ed gives us some inkling of the total power old longstanding negative attachment roles can have and how they can lead to numbing addiction.

If enough attachment and trust can be built up in a group of recovering addicts, the story can have a happier ending. Another man or woman may share their own story of breaking through the wall of denial, and this may in turn help break through the newcomer's refusal to hit bottom, get real, face the facts, engage with a sponsor, and work the steps surrounded by a supportive group. Results: a new life and new feelings about oneself which may be more accurate and healthy than the ones taken on while growing up.

Steps 4,5,6,7,8,9,and 10 provide guidance to gradually, repeatedly, and without judgment… taking a look at ourselves. It is only then that new growth can occur. The sponsor is fully equipped to help with the steps, not because of education, but because of personal experience with the steps and familiarity with the program.

Often a skilled professional is needed…one who understands emotions.

But the 12Step group itself functions as a holding environment, with members sharing their own struggles and victories and then listening in turn quietly to the next person who is prompted to tell about his or her own experience, strength and hope.

The spirit of anonymity provides a buffer of privacy which encourages one to share from the heart. Knowing that the rule of anonymity is present reduces the risk of gossip.

We don't repeat the words of others since we don't want our own repeated.

Somewhat like the EEG machine, the meetings somehow regulate our heart rate, slow down our breathing, and calm our minds into clearer thinking.

Through this new and accepting attachment situation, we find ourselves less disorganized and insecure, slowly working ourselves finally into what we understand to be a 'secure' feeling, and life improves while addiction fades.

Notes or Thoughts

Chapter

The ACE Study
and Addiction

O ne eye-opening result of research is called the Adverse Childhood
Experiences Study, or the ACE Study.

The original study was conducted by Kaiser Permanente from 1995
to 1997 with two separate sets of data collection from over 17,000 HMO
members in Southern California getting physical examinations and
completing confidential surveys concerning their childhood experiences
plus current health status and behaviors.

The Center for Disease Control and Prevention joined in this effort
and also looked at the incidence of ten separate categories of painful
circumstances. Some of these were : family violence, parental divorce,
drug or alcohol abuse in the family, death of a parent, and physical or
sexual abuse.

These researchers concluded that nearly two-thirds of injection
drug use can be attributed to abusive and traumatic childhood events.

Close correlation was found between painful childhood events and
addiction.

In a group I ran as a counselor at Freedom House in Chapel Hill
NC, one young woman, addicted to Percoset medication for pain,
shared that she had seen 'PawPaw blow his brains out' as a child.

Another person described how she and her younger two siblings had
been sent off by her teenaged mother in New York City to a relative
in New Orleans who beat them when they let up on the daily chores

of sweeping, cleaning, washing, cooking, and feeding the pigs and chickens.

She still had dreams at night of those beatings at the age of fifty.

When she finally made it back to New York, she was sexually abused by her cousins.

It is not wise to make a blanket statement about all who are addicted.

But the statistics are too high to deny tha a great many addicts suffered emotional and often physical pain during childhood.

People who have experienced both physical and sexual abuse are at least twice as likely to be using drugs than those who have experienced either abuse alone.

With alcohol, those who had suffered sexual abuse were three times more likely to start drinking in adolescence than those who had not.

For each emotionally traumatic childhood incident, there was a two-to threefold increase in the likelihood of alcohol abuse.

The ACE researchers reported, "Overall, these studies provide evidence that stress and trauma are common factors associated with consumption of alcohol at an early age as a means to self-regulate negative or painful emotions."

Addiction is a costly part of our daily national life, and not only in dollars

Accidents, deaths, loss of time on the job, hospitalization, neglect of children, crime and many other things can and do stem from the disease of addiction.

The Center for Disease Control and Prevention is naturally involved in this type of research.

When we know more about what causes any certain condition we can come closer to addressing the conditions that bring it into being.

I am reminded of a story told at a mental health conference that brings this point home.

It seems that a group was gathered at one point beside a river where parts of bodies were being rescued and the focus was on trying to restore them to wholeness.

Finally, someone noted that the best way to address the problem was to instead investigate what was happening up river to sever the limbs and try to deal with that. We are beginning to see some kind of prevention mentality currently.

In the field of addiction and treatment, we seem to be moving very slowly toward the painful but fruitful task of bringing to light some of the conditions and feelings which underlie almost all types of addictive behavior, and which are most often buried so deeply that they remain unconscious. We have no remembrance of our earliest 'programming', but we self-medicate because our pain remains, and plays out in our day to day life, until somehow we feel safe enough to recognize it.

One man shared in a meeting that he had been unable to learn to read, and still bore the marks of that shame and ostracism.

Tall as a boy, he was placed with much younger children, and teased because he could not read. Now in his 40's and sober, he shares that he will soon begin a program at the local community college. Being able to speak about his fear and self-doubt openly to an accepting group of twenty other recovering folks provided the support and courage needed to face and overcome his apprehensions. Afterwards, different ones shook his hand, gave him a hug, or offered an encouraging word. They know that the same would be done for them. Connection.

Great emphasis is put on helping the other fellow in the 12Step programs. It is called service, and it is counted as one of the very important ways to sustain recovery from alcohol, drugs, and other addictive behaviors.

Notes or Thoughts

Chapter

9

Freud's Addiction

Sigmund Freud (1856-1939), an Austrian neurologist, discovered several things which are very pertinent if we are to understand addiction.

His clients were puzzling to him at first, but he developed a treatment called by some 'the talking cure'.

He found that by listening deeply to the client's talking, many things which had been relegated to the unconscious slowly slipped out and were released from emotional pain by the pathway of language.

Freud lived and worked during the Victorian era, notorious for sexual repression and deeply denied and hidden sexual abuse as an outlet.

When Freud tried to explain what he had found out from his patients to the 'fathers' in Vienna medical circles, he felt an icy cold denial and more than a hint of rejection which caused him to quickly revise some of his theories. We don't know if Freud's own unconscious fears around his own father's actions played a part in this revision or not. Some speculate about this. It appears to me that Freud never dealt fully with his own repressions, despite his undisputed intellectual genius.

He continued to develop his 'talking cure' however, and smoked more and more as he listened and thought about each specific case.

Freud's method was called in German 'soul analysis', or psycho-analysis.

The striking thing about Freud's theory which pertains to addiction is the basic concept of the unconscious. Very important feelings and thoughts lay buried in us without our conscious knowledge of them, controlling our lives like an unseen captain guiding the wheel of a ship bound for unknown destinations.

Freud patiently listened, most often smoking a cigar as he tried to detect patterns in each unfolding narrative. Was the constant act of smoking a way to numb his own buried emotional pain as he listened to that of others? Perhaps it was.

Many of Freud's discoveries live on in the counseling and psychiatry of today.

With the dangers of World War II for Jews swirling around him, Freud escaped to London, but by this time cancer of the throat and palate from smoking had left him disfigured and disheartened. But he would not give up his addictive cigars.

Finally, ravaged by the results of a smoking habit which he adamantly refused to give up, Freud asked his doctors and his daughter to let him die. Read the details in The Violet Hour by Katie Roiphe, and your eyes will be opened.

No one of us could deny the brilliance of Sigmund Freud and his discoveries, or his pre-eminent place in the history of science. The name will never be forgotten. His methods and discoveries continue to astound us. But what about his 'soul'?

What do we know about the modification of any of Freud's repressions?

To my knowledge, Freud never had anyone he trusted for his own soul-analysis. He wrote 'The Interpretation of Dreams', but self-analyzing his own dreams was not the same as sitting down with another caring person who listens and resonates with our pain, allowing it to slowly surface and begin to heal.

Freud's followers were later able to discover that, from the matrix of the mother – child bond we can learn about deep attachment and communication with another, and begin to revise negative patterns as we talk and listen to the repressions we learn to see and accept in the emotional presence of another human being.

In the 12Step programs, as in outside counseling, the basic tool for recovery is this 'talker and listener' dyad.

Read anything by Peter Fonagy, who calls this 'mentalization', and describes it as one person trying to get a handle on the mindset of another. A 12Step meeting is built around listening and sharing, learning how our repressions rule us and how we can use certain tools to break through denial to 'a new freedom and a new happiness'.

Addiction comes about when some substance or behavior is used to cover over an emotional pain which is too great to bear. But we sometimes continue to use and abuse dangerous substances, often leading us to our death, wherein the repressed anguish is finally silenced, once and for all time.

Frequently, the repressed material is revealed as some form of stress overtakes us, and we crack open.

Richard Berendzen, former president of American University, gives us an account of this in his fascinating book, Come Here.

His childhood sexual trauma had never been mentioned to a soul, not even his wife.

With the growing obligations and increasing duties as AU's president, Berendzen took on more and more responsibilities, working overtime and on weekends until he finally snapped under the pressure.

Mentally and physically exhausted, he suddenly began making inappropriate phone calls in response to ads offering childcare in a woman's home. He would ask how sexual matters were handled.

Finally, a police officer's wife who kept children grew alarmed and Berendzen's phone was tapped as she kept him on the line. AU was notified about this.

Berendzen was removed from his office, sent to treatment at Johns Hopkins, and brought to a painful uncovering of the facts and feelings around his buried experiences of childhood sexual trauma. Like an erupting volcano, repressed material had broken through his denial, destroying his hitherto stellar presidency at AU.

Notes or Thoughts

Chapter

Tradition Five

I f we look carefully, the 12 Step programs address the basic problem which so many of us suffer from. Suffering is the key word here.

It is sometimes described as being a round peg in a square hole.

This position is extremely painful, and we reach out for our addictions to numb this suffering because we cannot get to the root of it.

Most often it is un-named and un-known to us, except that it hurts so badly.

In the terms of geometry, something is incongruent.

This foreign-to-us position makes us so angry, resentful, fearful, doubtful, or full of grief, that we plunge into addiction, or depression to cover up, even for a moment, the fact that things are so painfully not right. A round peg is in a square hole screams out for some form of addiction, and keeps going to it over and over, even to death.

Some of us say this untenable position is a sign that our spiritual connection to others and to ourselves, and to the Universe, is terribly askew.

The 12Step programs tell us that we are thereby negatively affected in a physical, mental, social, and spiritual way, and offers a program of help that is given freely to all, regardless of age, race, gender, education, nationality, or handicap.

The long form of Tradition Five states:

Each Alcoholics Anonymous group ought to be a spiritual entity, having but one primary purpose, that of carrying its message to the alcoholic who still suffers.

We cannot unearth the roots of our pain by ourselves, but in the all-inclusive, supportive circle of 12Steppers, with the help of our very own sponsor and the steps, we slowly make progress getting right shaped, and right sized, gradually fitting into our own skin more comfortably and breathing more easily. This is the recovery process.

It may be helpful to go over actual stories of addiction as we try to understand.

Let me tell you about Terry, a black man who is five months sober on his second try at AA recovery.

In Philly, as a teenager, he drank a lot of alcohol, freebased cocaine, and smoked marijuana, while also selling drugs which he told me was 'lucrative'. To quote Terry, 'I got tore up as a teen'. He says he also had experience as a gangbanger.

At 18 he enlisted in the Army.

He wanted a different scene and he wanted to protect his country, but he admits that enlisting was about the only thing going on. It was the 'easy way out'.

One other statement seemed very revealing to me.

Terry said that in the service, if you could not breathe, or if you were bleeding and dying, people would try to help you regardless of your race.

Reading between the lines, it is easy to imagine that this 'black man', as he calls himself, had experienced many instances when he was considered worthless because of the color of his skin. As another black youth told me, a person of color sometimes feels that' he does not belong on this earth'.

From 1983 until 2011 Terry was sent from conflict to conflict as a soldier.

Alcohol was plentiful and cheap, and the 'euphoria' or reward worked for years.

Whatever was bothering him, alcohol 'blocked it out'.

Two tours in Iraq, however, sent Terry into a diagnosis of PTSD.

As Terry sat before me, a strong wiry man with rippling muscles, his face softened and he glanced down at the floor.

Regaining his composure, he said…'the smell of burning bodies… death and destruction…an exploding IED and people GONE…'

We broke for coffee and a chance to breathe.

Terry's alcoholism continued until he went through two different rehabs, but he 'went back out' in 2011 due to marital stress, retiring from the service in March of the year 2011.

However, his connection and attachment in the AA fellowship are apparent.

His current recovery seems stable.

He has an excellent sponsor.

He attends meetings almost daily, sharing with the group what is going on.

He takes part, reading when asked, especially HOW IT WORKS.

He socializes with other members, young and old, whatever color, a friend to all, joking at the coffee pot.

His nightmares, depression, and anxiety are treated with medication.

Best of all, his youngest and closest son, in the same town, gets to be with his newly sober father.

Terry says, 'I am not making any broken promises. I am trying to show by my actions that I am living a new life so my kid can see that for himself.'

Terry's attachment to the 12Step program is paying off in healthy attachments to others, and to himself. In the words of AA, this is a spiritual awakening. Terry is remarkable for giving and getting a lot of hugs and handshakes.

Notes or Thoughts

Chapter

11

Talking and Listening

As I sat and listened to Terry tell his story of addiction, change, and points of recovery, a certain calmness came over me.

Here was a man I knew from the meeting, and I was trying to understand the trajectory of his life, plus the current state of his recovery from drugs and alcohol.

I could picture him repairing cars, doing a brake job, with a son thirty years younger who had been born on his very own exact birthday.

One of the tragedies of addiction is the fact of ruined relationships, where the importance of substances or behaviors took precedent over everything else.

Terry wants to put something new in place of the way his son saw him before, always drinking. Rather than words and promises, he is relying on actions.

He emphasized the repeated new experience of working together, father and son, without the constant need of alcohol to keep going.

Terry knows somehow that only repeated sober companionship could begin to lessen and finally erase the memories of him as a drunken father from his son's mind.

And the 12 Step programs reminds him of how to do this, one day at a time.

As for me, listening and absorbing Terry's story was healing.

Having ended my own primary addiction, I was now able to pause and pay full attention to another human being, aware of our bond, 'being there' for him.

I think this had come about through the great 12Step emphasis on connection.

Other members, sponsors, sponsees, meeting leaders, and phone buddies had provided, over and over, that human connection that I had lost somehow, and had instead filled in with an ever-increasing addiction to alcohol.

Previously, my time and thought was taken up with my addictions, and listening carefully to another was well-nigh impossible.

But here I sat, without being pulled by the frantic need to cover my own pain, face to face with another person, calm and attentive, 'being there' in quietness, listening.

This was all the result of so many small actions of connection the program suggests.

I had learned to make coffee and done that many times.

I had learned how to set up the meeting and done that often.

I had led the meeting over and over again.

I had made an attempt to speak to the newcomers.

I had given a hug to those picking up chips for time accomplished: the white chip for starting or restarting, yellow for 30 days, red for 90 days, blue for six months, green for nine months, medallions for years up to 81.

I had worked with my sponsor on the 12 steps.

I had worked with sponsees on the 12 steps.

I had continued to read the literature.

I had learned to really pray, asking for guidance all during my day.

All the things that had been suggested I made an attempt to do, knowing my recovery and my sobriety depended on it.

And here I was, at last.

I could listen and be present to another human being.

This was an earthshaking change for me.

Gone was that cold isolation from myself and others.

In its place was connection and togetherness and a new place in the Universe.

Terry and I laughed and cried with each other.

We looked each other in the eye and both of us understood new things.

We knew and understood about coming out of the pain of addiction and loneliness into the 'sunshine of the spirit'.

We had done things the program suggested, and found that they worked.

We both were experiencing a new and exciting kind of life.

There was no clear explanation about how this thing worked, only a definite experience that it DID work, if we followed 12Step directions.

We had both had a prior life of addiction that was killing us.

Now we sat together talking, sober for only one day at a time.

A mystery and a miracle for Sue and for Terry, thanks to AA.

And that connection held to other people in the program, as I began to listen and hear what each one said and also to notice changes coming about for them, slowly but surely if they stuck with it.

Getting to know others on a deeper level also may me realize that for many of us, the suffering had begun many years earlier.

Let me try to tell you about another friend I have made in the 12Step rooms.

Her name is Rochelle.

Notes or Thoughts

Chapter

Rochelle

W hen I first met Rochelle at a 12 Step meeting, her name was Rock.

Giving up the suffering that came with alcoholism was the first thing. But the second thing was gradually uncovering the suffering and pain that came with gender diffusion.

Rock was tall and very solidly built and had served in the Marines for some years with great outward success.

But in addition to alcoholism, suicidal feelings repeatedly crept in.

Finally Rock found a therapist who worked with Gender Dysphoria, a condition in which the patient struggles to find a comfortable place on the gender continuum.

Gradually, we became aware of small changes in Rock. His curly hair began to grow longer and he was sporting earrings.

He was perfectly honest as he shared about the difficulties he was facing.

Honesty is one of the bedrock requirements in any 12Step program, as is the emphasis on anonymity, which allows one to BE honest.

Rock asked for help from the women in the program with matters of style.

Soon, a pedicure, paint, and attractive sandals transformed Rock's feet.

One day, when identifying himself in the opening circle, Rock changed his name and now is called Rochelle.

My unforgettable event with Rochelle was at a local vigil held soon after the Orlando massacre at the Pulse nightclub in June 2016.

I wanted to go to the vigil and show my support as a straight person, but the shooting and violence were so fresh in my mind that I was absolutely full of fear.

Knowing that I had to break through that fear, I spoke to Rochelle at a meeting and asked her to go with me, and she agreed.

After the Orlando shooting, everyone felt fear.

Rochelle wore her long curly hair down, and looked great in a skirt topped by a black tee shirt which read: Be Calm...TRANSGENDER!

The crowded vigil was held outside at a gay bar in town, and so I went in and got a ginger ale.

When I waved my credit card, the bartender smiled and shook his head. "Nope", he whispered.

"We take care of our friends".

We heard speakers in English and in Spanish.

We heard from people of all ages and descriptions.

We heard about fear and hate and hostility.

But the resilience of the human spirit was palpable and present among the fluttering rainbow flags and the dancing candle flames as we stood under the stars, roped off and guarded by the police.

What a night.

I knew that Rochelle had struggled with her gender issues for many years.

The acceptance, love, and companionship in the 12Step rooms had provided her at last with a 'family' who only wanted her to be her deepest true self as she went through this difficult transition... while other segments of society opened fire.

AA was a circle, holding hands, and Rochelle was a vital and vibrant part of that circle, her wide smile a reminder that each of us counted, no matter what.

Acceptance is probably the most basic healing ingredient in 12Step recovery.

We are invited to come in and the only requirement is that we admit we are addicted.

First of all, that addiction is to alcohol, substances, or negative behavioral patterns.

But as we progress, we find with astonishment that we also are addicted to holding on to that suffering we feel as we cling desperately to an out-dated and painful attachment position sometimes begun in childhood in order to please and pacify our parents, to fit in, to be what we 'should' be.

These are the wonderful unforeseen changes we see in the rooms.

And as we connect deeply with many different others, we can feel our growing connection within our own true self, left behind in fragments long ago, when we were unable to master wholeness.

Notes or Thoughts

Chapter

Neuroscience

How does acceptance and connection tie in with neuroscience? First of all, we are mammals.

Jaak Panksepp, in The Archaeology of Mind, gives us a fascinating reminder that our brains have evolved from a cold-blooded separated reptile state into a necessary mammalian togetherness designed to protect and nourish us from birth until death.

We still have that ancient primitive brain to perform certain functions as needed.

But it is the limbic system that makes us human, and binds us to other mammals.

Our limbic system is the apparatus that makes us who we are.

We have two great driving forces: first to survive, then to reproduce.

Each of us is human in our own unique way...one of a kind.

And for each of us, acceptance and connection are absolutely necessary both to survive and to produce children.

Panksepp delineates complicated sets of behaviors which have evolved to support our two basic drives, but above all is the limbic system, our mammalian inheritance.

We are creatures created for connection, togetherness, and acceptance.

And of all the animals, our young stay dependent the longest, remaining in need of the family for a remarkable period of time.

Freud's followers found that first the mother, then others, were crucial to provide the first and most basic emotional regulation for the helpless human infant.

The mother, or another caretaking individual, 'listened' and paid attention to the baby's signals and cries, guessing what attention or act was needed.

This was the beginning of an individual attachment pattern which went on until the child grew to independence and carried on that unconscious pattern into his or her own life, for better or worse.

One startling example comes from Romania. When their brutal dictator was ousted after forcing women to have more babies, the orphanages were full and overflowing. In the '80s and '90s these institutions warehoused large roomfuls of cribs crowded together, row after row. These infants were fed a propped bottle, but had little or no interaction with overworked women struggling to simply keep the orphanage clean.

The brains of these children did not mature properly and many developed RAD, Reactive Attachment Disorder.

Because the orphans had not experienced the normal attachment, connection, and communication on a repeated daily basis, many of their brains were disordered.

Another example of mammalian attachment comes from Harry Harlow's monkeys.

In an experiment, Harlow tested baby monkeys to check on attachment.

Wire 'mothers' were constructed, one plain with a bottle of milk, the other with a terry cloth covering but no milk.

The baby monkeys chose the terry cloth mother they could attach and cling to.

We mammals need the presence of our mothers when young.

We need our emotions of fear, anger, grief, and even joy regulated by her more mature limbic system until we can slowly learn to self-regulate.

Just as we need food and water to grow physically, we need the give and take of attachment to become emotionally mature.

And sometimes that give and take can be lacking or problematic.

But, without help we are unable to discern our old buried ways of interacting.

We continue to learn through interactions until we leave our family of origin.

I am reminded of Olivia.

I met Olivia in AA some time ago.

It was only when we had established a deep and trusting relationship that I heard about her attachment pattern.

Olivia was 8 and her sister was 6 when the trauma occurred.

The parents were going out and so they engaged a baby sitter for the girls.

However, at the last minute, this baby sitter was unable to show up and hurriedly called a teenaged boy from her high school to fill in.

That night, while Olivia was watching TV, she heard her younger sister scream from the other room.

Rushing through the door, Olivia caught sight of the baby sitter exposing himself to her little sister.

Shocked by a sight she had never seen before herself, Olivia grabbed her sibling and soothed her the best that she could as an eight year old.

The event was never processed due to shame and secrecy, and Olivia's sister had many emotional repercussions, always with Olivia comforting and taking care of her. On the playground and elsewhere, Olivia could not fully relax. She was now locked into an attachment pattern which demanded that she always look out for and save her sister. This pattern continued into adulthood.

Alcohol numbed these turbulent feelings of powerlessness for Olivia, which were created long ago at 8 years old.

Notes or Thoughts

Chapter

Punishment and Compassion

M aia Szalavitz, in her book 'Unbroken Brain: A Revolutionary New Way of Understanding Addiction' calls for more compassion in treatment methods and attitudes.

Rather than punishment by society, and self-punishment by the addict, she tells of her own recovery from drugs which took place without harsh rehabs or the prayer, surrender to a higher power, confession, and restitution prescribed by the 'steps'.

Hers is one of the current new views of addiction.

She calls addiction a learning disability involving the brain's reward system.

Szalavitz describes growing up with a hyper-reactive nervous system that constantly made her feel overwhelmed, alienated and unlovable. (One wonders how that came about.) Heroin gave her a sense of comfort, safety, and love that she couldn't get from other people. Her parents could not understand what had finally happened to their 'gifted' child who had always excelled academically.

But intellectual excellence cannot save us from addiction. She recommends cognitive behavioral therapy and motivational enhancement for recovery and her point is well taken.

But let me tell you about Mike.

Mike has been in and out of the 12Step program for years.

He grew up on the outskirts of Wilmington NC and has been in several rehabs, always going back to alcohol after having periods of sobriety.

Mike and I happened to both came early to a meeting and while nobody else was around, we were able to connect and talk freely and openly.

At one point, he hesitantly revealed that he was now actually homeless.

I shared with him that I was writing a book exploring attachment difficulties in the lives of alcoholics, explaining that my opinion on this subject might be controversial.

So, we had each dropped down to reveal some of our own vulnerabilities.

The room was very quiet and peaceful and the only sound was rain on the roof.

I explained that I thought early painful events or trauma in a child's life could be a precursor to addiction.

Mike's hair was combed neatly, and he wore jeans and a T-shirt. I wondered how he managed 'on the streets', but realized this was just curiosity on my part and allowed the thought to fade away, unspoken.

But I did ask him about his childhood.

Without any hesitation he said his mother had been diagnosed with breast cancer when he was twelve and she was in agonizing pain until her death two years later as he turned fourteen. He could not forget the gruesome surgeries.

In his rural, very conservative area, there were no counseling services for a boy whose mother was dying, and adults in the family did not talk about feelings.

So Mike was left with anger and hate toward a God who would take his mother away from him in such a cruel manner. Resentment coursed through his body.

We know his age was a crucial factor, since the beginning years of puberty around 12 to 14 are an age when the child needs to feel parental support as he or she begins the process of becoming an adult. Bewildering changes come about, and a youngster depends on the anchoring presence of the parents to make a safe emotional passage.

As far as I know, Mike had never really examined his feelings thoroughly.

The time for the meeting grew closer, and I excused myself and thanked Mike, getting his permission to use his story in my book.

The time had come for me to lead the meeting, and I invited Mike to sit at the table to my right, rather than in the back corner by the door.

But after the members began to share, I noticed the chair was empty and that Mike was gone.

When the one hour of meeting was up, the group held hands in a circle and ended with the Serenity Prayer.

Walking out through the parlor, I suddenly realized that Mike had never left the building, but had chosen to remain quietly by himself there, in thought.

Maybe I had overstepped and intruded.

Maybe old feelings had been stirred up.

Unlike women, men are socialized never to reveal 'soft' emotions.

But the powerful connection I had felt between us was unmistakable.

And Mike's story had strengthened my belief that addiction could be, for some, a necessary numbing mechanism for events and feelings in the past which were too great to bear alone. Events and feelings which it was necessary to 'forget'.

I have unshakable faith in the 12 Step programs.

Meetings have sustained me in places as far away as Singapore and as near as the next small town.

They are absolutely free, and have no other requirement other than to identify oneself as an alcoholic or an addict of some description.

And they foster connection and attachment in so many ways, large and small, in order for us to look at our patterns of engagement, with the help of the middle steps.

Notes or Thoughts

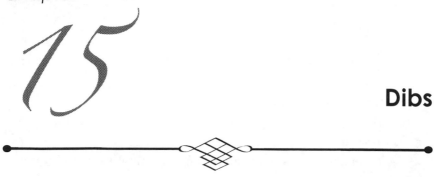

Chapter

15

Dibs

Perhaps the one book which best illustrates the power of the right brain and the limbic system for connection and attachment is Dibs In Search of Self by Virginia Axline.

The story begins with a little boy at a school for young children who never talks, and who exhibits bizarre behavior, to the consternation of his concerned and puzzled teachers.

Dibs is dropped off and picked up by the chauffeur, often refusing to enter the car and crying to stay at school until he is placed bodily in the front seat, and the car door is shut.

We find that both parents of the child are brilliant and famous scientists, and the mother wonders if Dibs might be retarded, asking the school personnel to observe and give their opinion, in case she needs to send him off somewhere.

Her only caveat is that she herself never be interviewed.

Virginia Axline is called in for what turns out to be classic play therapy once a week with this troubled child, in a special room at school full of playthings.

When faced with paint or crayons, Dibs at first will only read the name of the manufacturer, or spell out the color on the label. Other revelations come when the little boy, warming up to his therapist, reads to her with an ability far beyond his years. When emotional, Dibs goes back again to the left brain puzzles for safety.

At one session he asks anxiously if his therapist is going to lock the door, pleading in the language of a much younger and more emotional 'self', NO LOCK DOORS.

The little boy never uses the pronoun 'I', but instead says,' Dibs will do this, or Dibs will do that'.

Gradually, his therapist makes progress and Dibs improves somewhat.

The mother is called in, and weeps when she hears that Dibs is not impaired intellectually.

She agrees to a conference with Axline.

It turns out that these parents never wanted a child since their careers came first.

The pregnancy was a shock and disappointment to them both.

When Dibs was very small, every toy, book, and puzzle imaginable was bought for him, and he was locked in his room alone to develop only what we might call left brain capabilities.

His only really warm relationship was with Jake the gardener.

When a favorite and wonderful tree outside his window had to be cut down, Dibs cried out to Jake, and the gardener managed to bring one branch back to the boy, who kept it safely in his room.

Axline's descriptions of the play sessions reveal the slow give and take of emotions that occur between the two over a period of time.

As Dibs slowly masters some of the right brain victories with the help of his therapist, he gains a more solid sense of self, and begins to refer to himself as 'I'.

And as the child unfolds more fully, so does the mother.

She is able to get in touch with her own emotions, and enter into a relationship with Dibs that includes more than simply the intellectual, and they both thrive.

Finally, 'father' also visits the school one day.

My descriptions can only hint at the power of this book.

What it says to me is that the development of the left brain, or rational intellect, is necessary for our ongoing lives, but it is the right brain and limbic system which may truly make us who we are. We are born for connection and must have it.

Dibs was missing some of the crucial attachment bonds that he would need to mature in a full and healthy manner.

However, once a week for an hour, he had had a speaking and listening experience with an skilled therapist that not only put him on the path to healing, but also brought his mother out of her own frozen emotions.

The story of Dibs illustrates just how strongly any child must adjust to parental expectations. Dibs adjusts to the rational expectations of his parents, but has a stunted emotional life as a result of this unhealthy position of attachment.

What happens to the youngster in a troubled family? That youngster meets the needs of his troubled family in order to survive and be taken care of, until he reaches his own maturity. All is relegated to the unconscious and forgotten by him. He is on automatic pilot with no immediate recollection of the implicit directions he is faithfully but unknowingly following. Many of us have had to uncover 'forgotten' templates, hidden away, but faithful to our needs for survival at any cost.

No pill or medical procedure can change the inevitable course of these directions, but, as in the case of Dibs, a deep experience of talking and listening can release some of the power of the skewed life trajectory, and permit healing to begin.

Stories from the 12Step rooms can provide examples of how the middle steps, with a sponsor, somehow provide the necessary ingredients to bring about insight into old patterns, and more than that, plant the seeds, sprouts, and blossoms of a new and more joyful life of attachment and connection within the supportive circle of the 12Step meetings and fellowship.

Notes or Thoughts

Chapter

16

Scaer and Levine

Robert Scaer MD has worked as a physician with insurance companies and noted in reviewing motor vehicle accidents there was sometimes a very marked contrast between the intense severity of symptoms in his client and the relatively innocuous low speed of the vehicle at the time of injury. This was a puzzle.

Insurance companies saw this phenomenon as an attempt at secondary gain, or payoff, by the injured party.

With further investigation, however, Scaer found that in many cases there had been a prior trauma at a vulnerable age which at the time of the incident was then bodily recalled by the emotional impact of the motor vehicle accident.

One woman, brutally raped at sixteen, experienced severe repercussions after the impact of a crash at a mere five miles an hour. Fear had taken her back in time.

Scaer continues to delve deeply into neuroscience, discovering more and more about the fact that unprocessed trauma in the past could be triggered by mild 'wrecks' in the present, since the body holds those old memories for survival.

Scaer's book, The Body Bears the Burden, gives us fascinating accounts of this. And Peter Levine, PhD adds a fascinating bit in Waking Tiger, reminding us that in the animal kingdom, where there is no language such as ours, an antelope will shake out the nervous system after a long and intense flight from the lion, trembling until a calmer state is reached approaching normality. In a video of a fleeing zebra, we can see that the animal is COMPLETING his running. But we resolve our fears by talking.

Evidence that talking about intense human feelings to attentive listeners can bring some kind of closure, or processing is apparent in the sharings within the rooms.

Just recently, I sat in a meeting of about 30 people next to a woman named Caroline.

As the meeting progressed, I noticed that Caroline had tears flowing down her cheeks but she was wordless. She tightly contained her feelings, which leaked out in silent weeping.

She wiped away the tears with one hand in an attempt to gain back control.

She seemed to be overcome with wordless emotions.

People were sharing, but she was caught in the grip of emotional pain.

Finally, I leaned over to her and whispered, 'Consider sharing'.

At the next opportunity, she did just that, sobbing.

She shared that her best friend was now dying...

Then she mentioned the names of several key persons who had died during a short period in her childhood.

Finally she put her head in her hands, and sobbed, 'They all LEAVE'.

The roomful of people became totally quiet.

No rustle of paper.

No coughing.

Not a sound.

She had been heard by all of us, and all of us had received her pain.

Gradually she regained her composure, and the meeting began once more.

I accidentally dropped my glasses, picked them up and shot her a grin.

Blowing her nose and wiping her cheeks, she grinned back.

How close are tears and laughter!

I think this woman experienced relief and healing from engaging and sharing with the group.

She had an emotional burden which was unbearable, but the connection and acceptance in the room allowed her to share rather than bottle up her grief.

She was able to get it out, talking to us while in emotional pain, tears flowing.

And we were able to just quietly listen.

This is 12Step healing.

Notes or Thoughts

Chapter

Allan Schore

In his book, Affect Regulation and the Origin of the Self, Allan Schore reveals the fact that the interaction between mother and infant indelibly 'sets the stage' for every aspect of the baby's internal and external functioning throughout the lifespan.

As the mother, or primary caretaker, interacts with the newborn, her brain and her affect regulation serve to regulate his, and thus a 'self' begins to develop.

If the mother is deeply depressed or mentally challenged, the baby does not get this 'presence', and may later in life be depressed himself.

The mother and child are almost constantly exchanging signals back and forth. These could be visual, looks and glances, or sounds, sighs and murmurs. Also these signals could be transmitted through touch.

Young babies will exhibit panic and distress when presented with a 'still face'.

This occurs when the maternal figure relaxes and freezes her face, staring elsewhere with no movement or sound, totally ignoring her offspring. The child, depending on her mother for regulation (soothing touch and a soft lullaby bringing down fussiness into slumber) shows concern and actively signals, frantically seeking t re-establish bonding and interaction.

For some addicted persons, the drink or drug may provide a numbing of painful forgotten states experienced long ago which surface under stress.

If the addicted man or woman stops drinking or drugging without working the steps with a sponsor, this pain from a forgotten past event may drive them back to their substances, because the helplessness of childhood and youth remain around that pain, and it feels insurmountable. Consequently, we turn again to addiction.

Because, in the past, children were thought to 'forget' negative states, many of us were ignored as the adults scurried to cover up drinking in the family, or smooth over the death or illness of a parent, or consider normal placing the ten year old daughter as surrogate mother to several other siblings, stealing her young life.

The survival part of our brain notes these events and 'capsules in' the anguish, contained and hidden until it can be re-opened years later.

And, as the capsule is finally opened, the contents pour out with all the helplessness and fear of the original child, until the pain is finally heard.

I experienced incest with my inebriated (and perhaps himself sexually abused as a child) father at age four, but was told by my mother that this was NEVER to be mentioned again, and that it could NOT have happened. So...

I hurt many people as I attempted to 'forget', dissociating my feelings and memories, doing whatever was necessary to avoid thoughts of suicide.

No one could find an explanation or decipher the buried secret. So...

My life was out of control in many ways.

These memories are coded in our bodily systems, 'forgotten' as we are commanded, but remembered in so many unconscious ways as we try desperately to stay on keel, attempting in every way possible to look normal and appear to be 'happy'.

We are created for survival, and our survival brain will make it possible to bury experiences which are too much for us, but they can finally be laid bare, with all the original fear, anger, and pain felt by the young person long ago.

Because the anguish of the original situation is so overwhelming, Mother Nature has found a way to carry us forward behind a mask of sanity (The Mask of Sanity by Hervey Cleckley) in hopes that we may reproduce and carry on the species.

While there are many treatments and protocols, it is my belief and experience that the 12 Steps, if worked in the right spirit with another recovering person, can begin to pry open the capsule. Attachment patterns can be changed and healed.

The shock and pain of the origina but now- hidden emotional position we had to take for survival can finally be investigated and explored if we have engaged the recovery fellowship of attachment, care, and acceptance through the 12 Step programs or another means of supportive others who understand and accept us.

Notes or Thoughts

Chapter

Princess Diana

Princess Diana would seem on the surface to have been securely attached in childhood, with her bulimia just a pampered woman's silliness.

However, as we look more closely at her beginnings, we see underlying tensions in the family which may have led to turbulent internal emotional storms.

Born into a noble British line, she suffered from the needs of her father to bring forth a male heir with his wife, Frances, to inherit the wealth and lands of earldom.

Two sisters were born, one after another.

Disappointment.

A son, John, came along.

Elation.

John died as a tiny infant.

Bitter disappointment.

Diana was born.

Complete and utter determination to have a male heir.

Frances was sent off to uncover what the 'problem' could be, and she grew intensely resentful and hostile over this indignity of scrutiny by doctors.

She finally did give birth to a boy, Charles, but sought and gained a divorce when Diana was 7.

The children remained with their father, and Frances remarried.

Under older assumptions, Diana would just ignore and forget these deep tensions during her growing up years, and live happily ever after with no remembrances.

However, her 'self' had been forged in a cauldron of emotional pain created by the extremely strong feelings between her parents over having a son.

Diana had a certain amount of confidence, but lurking underneath her beauty probably lay unresolved and unheard attachment issues of 'being less than' which were exacerbated by the discovery of her husband's preference for Camilla.

If Bowlby's colleagues are correct, her tenuous attachment to her mother and father was repeated in her severed attachment to her husband.

The pattern had been set.

The pattern was unconsciously repeated.

No, you may say.

She was just a spoiled young woman.

She was immature and never grew up.

She should have controlled her bulimia.

Children DO NOT take in or remember these things.

But we can begin to see that perhaps some of these emotional pressures in childhood really do leave their mark.

That is why the 12Step programs have a very strong emphasis on 'not judging', and looking at others with compassion, rather than faulting them.

We are warned that other people have their own issues we cannot understand.

We are repeatedly asked to be compassionate toward other.

We are reminded that 'love and tolerance is our code'.

Most of all, we experience over and over the acceptance and connection the program offers us, which we are reminded to extend to others.

Unconditional welcome, as we give it to others, is then felt in full measure by ourselves, freeing us to be more alive, more joyful.

And, because the program is open to all, we have the opportunity to practice connection with a remarkably wide variety of folks we might never have met in former circles.

We learn in the shares people offer.

Other lives, other pain, other ways of being.

And this Higher Power is suddenly present as never before.

We cannot 'prove' it, but we can feel it in flashes, as surely as one can 'feel' the wonder and mystery of the stars against the dark night sky.

This is not an analytical, left brain 'proof'.

Blaise Pascal said it well. (translation from the French)

'The heart has its reasons that reason knows not.'

The right brain is set up to discern wholeness and connection.

The left brain is set up to analyze and separate one thing from another.

We need both hemispheres of course.

But we need desperately to finally feel part of a whole, to find our designated place.

The 12Steps and the fellowship help us find our designated place, a place in which we finally feel comfortable and useful, 'fitting' for us, so to speak.

Where we once were out of place and dying, now we live and continue recovering, in a new place exactly our size and shape, that fits.

Notes or Thoughts

Chapter

Bill W. and Dr. Bob

I t is helpful to re-examine the start of AA and the 12 Step programs by looking back to what was going on in the time leading up to 1935.

Bill W. had had many problems with his drinking, and his wife Lois, naturally,had tried to get him to stop many many times, to no avail. She tried everything.

Bill was entranced with the stock market; he captured a few brilliant successes and was let down by many failures. He may have felt he was destined to make a name for himself. But, drink was his nemesis.

Finally, his dance with alcohol landed him in the hospital one more time and the doctor, helpless, informed Bill and Lois that the next step was 'wet brain' and death.

Travelling to close one more deal, which eventually fell through, Bill found himself in a hotel, very despondent, staring at two signs.

One sign pointed to the bar, his usual recourse.

The other sign pointed the other way to the hotel desk, and featured a directory of nearby churches, some of which included meetings of The Oxford Group.

Bill knew The Oxford Group worked with alcoholics, so he called and got the name and number of a member, Dr. Bob.

These two met with each other, and the result was a get-together and talk which lasted until the wee hours of the morning.

We cannot guess the exact words they exchanged, but it takes little imagination to sense that an immediate connection and understanding took place that night.

As in many of the rooms all over the world today, these two men found themselves at the First Step...We admitted we were powerless over alcohol, and that our lives were unmanageable. Note the fact that two people together began the healing.

The word WE is the bedrock of AA, for it is finally in the company of another, and rarely alone, that we discover the basic ingredients needed to stop drinking.

It is also in the company and connection of others that we find w can explore and admit the terrible straits we have come to, and the depth of the shocking divide from our real selves that causes a pain so deep that numbing is the only solution.

When both Bill W. and Dr. Bob had stabilized in their newly found sobriety, the pure joy and relief they experienced (a reprieve from death) drove them to hospitals and street corners, seeking out any and every drunk they could find.

Tirelessly, they told their own stories and worked to exhaustion with other suffering alcoholics, never giving up until finally, slowly, others found they could quit drinking also with this strange new method of talking and listening, one to another.

The movement grew to other locations, and was praised by prominent men and organizations. Everyone was jubilant over the success of AA.

Tempted to go in the direction of profit and fame, AA instead wisely adopted the way of anonymity for all members, and a tradition of being 'not for sale'.

The Big Book of AA was written as a guide to sobriety, and a General Service Office was set up in New York as headquarters of what would become a world-wide organization which stretches around the world today.

There can be no quarrel that the 12 Steps of AA have worked for so many people.

And we might say 'why'?

It is my guess that the attachment, first and foremost, is crucial to the efficacy of the 12 Step programs. Ponder the slogan, 'Meeting makers make it'.

Also, let me cite the words of many who relapse and go back to drinking.

'I drifted away from AA and stopped going. Then I relapsed.'

One man's sponsor told him that it was the 'I' who relapses and drinks; it is the WE who remains in recovery, one day at a time, attached and connected.

As a tribute to the two founders, many a meeting room features the pictures of the two who started the fellowship out of a late-night sharing.

It was Dr. Bob, the anchor, who cautioned Bill to 'keep it simple'.

And ironically, it was Bill W., the billowing sail, who finally without realizing it made a name for himself, and is now known all over the world today as the man who started AA.

Any member honors his own anonymity by simply referring to himself as 'a friend of Bill W' when meeting another suspected alcoholic or addict.

Notes or Thoughts

Chapter

The Middle Steps

The real key to recovery is in working the steps, and particularly the middle steps. We are powerless over our addiction until we begin the uncovering that takes place while 'working the steps' which means applying them in our own lives and not just memorizing or becoming familiar with them. This takes a sponsor.

Working with a sponsor creates another level of intimacy and connection, and helps the sponsor herself (men with men, women with women) dig deeper into the steps.

The uncovering at first addresses the period of our addiction, where we are asked to be very honest about the things we did and the people we hurt, urging us to make lists of those we wronged, and discover appropriate ways to make amends.

Sharing this with another person once again reinforces the WE, and underlines the power of a newer and healthier attachment to another person as we are seen, naked in our admission of wrongdoings, and thereby gaining in true acceptance.

The acceptance, the honesty, the connection, the Promises (a description of the results of recovery) all, in a room full of addicted people, serve to move us from one step to another, gaining in the process our true selves, long hidden by addiction.

When sobriety really takes hold is through the sixth and seventh steps.

We are advised to list and examine our 'character defects' which at first are the manipulation and isolation of the addict with so many variations, but thereafter tend to include the misshapen poses we have adopted earlier in life to survive.

Through repeated runs through these steps, we gradually arrive at some kind of original position we begin to feel comfortable with, but which may alienate family and friends who need us to remain constant in old dysfunctional systems.

We learn how and when to make amends.

We learn to observe ourselves and try on new behaviors and attitudes.

We learn to see when we are wrong and promptly admit it.

We are asked to consider and recognize a Higher Power, which at first is the recovery group itself, which we feel enfolding us, accepting us, loving us.

These middle steps first remove guilt and shame around addiction, and the behaviors we exhibited. We shed some of our self-loathing.

Then the middle steps begin to reach deeper into our being, showing where we have become selfish, or afraid, or angry, or unforgiving, unable to grow and change.

And in removing some of these traits we thought were indelible, we begin to find some kind of original creation that reaches out to others and connects more wisely.

Suddenly, we are eager to help another addict work the steps and become changed.

We sponsor a newcomer, and the rewards are amazing.

So we sponsor another, and the payoffs are even greater as we learn that all we have to do is share our experience with the steps.

We are not responsible for getting someone sober.

Their recovery is up to them alone.

Our job is simply to share our experience with the steps and be a living reminder that the 12 steps not only bring sobriety from drugs and alcohol, but slowly give us a new and joyful attitude and a different way to live and connect.

We first have to latch on to the fellowship, which means doing the service work which ultimately glues us more closely to the group.

Then we must jump into the steps, not allowing doubt or fear to keep us from this, no matter how afraid we might be.

If we sit in the chair and listen, offer to read HOW IT WORKS, wash coffee cups, scrub the floor, we have made a beginning.

We must make an effort to greet the newcomer no matter how painful it may feel to us. The newcomer may be the one we see change in a startling manner.

Not just the newcomer who is similar in age, color, education, or culture, but indeed, those who seem starkly different.

We are beginning, in this way, to start new and healthy attachment patterns.

It feels strange at first, but slowly this new engagement begins to supersede the old crazy and painful one that we drank and drugged to numb away.

We are asked to offer connection.

We thereby gain connection.

Notes or Thoughts

Chapter

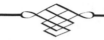

Maia Szalavitz

In her 2016 book, Unbroken Brain, Szalavitz gives us the shocking story of her own addiction, which took her to the end point of injecting heroin daily, combined with hits of cocaine... and then getting suspended from Columbia for dealing, followed by being indicted later for possession of 2.5 kilos of drugs.

She describes the court case which faced her, with a possibility of incarceration, for selling drugs and possessing this large amount of cocaine. Her divorced parents both had to put up their houses as bail to buy her some time.

She details the depressing methadone clinic she tries to attend, and tells of the shame and harsh judgment handed out along with the cup of orange 'dose'.

She lets us in on the very moment she finally feels tempted in desperation to seduce a friend's boyfriend she hardly knows in order to score drugs.

But, at this point she lets go and allows her mother to take her to detox and rehab.

The backstory of this addict gives us one more somewhat new idea to ponder.

Can a deep and lifelong depression in a parent affect a child? Could the severe depression of her father have had any effect on her, early in life?

At a young age Maia was diagnosed in nursery school with ADHD and given Ritalin for a short period. She remembers feeling unloved, alone, depressed.

Looking back, she detects possible signs of Asperger's on the autism syndrome.

She recounts several examples of trying to soothe herself by counting, rocking, or repeating the names of chemicals she saw in her father's lab.

A Holocaust survivor, her father suffered from deep depression.

Her mother develops cancer of the throat, and Maia makes drawings of the 'bump' which remained prominent after her mother undergoes surgery.

A pet dies at nursery school and thoughts of death take over her child's mind.

Maia uses rocking, counting, and other means in her attempt at affect regulation.

She has trouble with the give and take of relationships, and in the end finds that drugs numb it all out.

After a rocky growing up period where she does acid trips with a friend in high school, she finds herself attending Columbia, but ends up with track marks all over her body from shooting up, finally facing a suspended jail sentence.

Maia is perhaps another example of someone who turned to drugs as a way to numb the unbearable turmoil in her own mind.

She, like others, is put off by the prayer, forgiveness, and 'spiritual' aspect of the 12Step programs. But eventually, her time in the program turns into solid recovery and she is let off by the judge who sees clearly she is now physically and mentally a new person. We in the 12Step programs describe this as a spiritual awakening.

For many, and initially for myself, the apparent lack of 'substance' in the fellowship can be off-putting. We crave rational left brain analysis, and more intellectual dialogue.

I remember scoffing at the poker chips to mark time in sobriety.

The steps and traditions were printed on large window shades and hung on the wall, to my dismay.

The founders had no PhD after their names.

And the thirty people gathered for the meeting included a recognizable cross-section of society: all ages, sizes, occupations, races, and backgrounds.

Some stumbled as they tried to read out loud the Preamble, or the Promises.

How in the world could these drunks and addicts keep me sober!

But what kept me coming back was the honest shares and the palpable spirit of calm and serenity that inevitably spoke to me louder than the poker chips.

I learned that the 12Step programs had long ago broken away from the religious confines of churches and temples, soaring out from the bonds of theology to become universally 'spiritual', accepting everyone of any sort who sought sobriety.

Szalavitz tells her story well, revealing many of the indignities and name-calliing which increase the pain and humiliation already felt by every addicted person.

Her thesis is this: addiction is a disorder of learning.

My thesis is the same, except I believe it is a disorder of learning how to connect and attach and interact with others, often begun so far back it cannot even be recalled, only acted out painfully until we are able to 'wake up'.

Maia's wake-up call, probably, was facing a 15 year to life sentence in jail for possession.

In rehab, she had the experience of a new way of relating to herself and others, with the 12 Steps and a sponsor as guides. No self-help book can do that, because there we read the words alone. We need healthy human attachment bonds to heal.

We literally get a new experience, within the bonds of 12 Step connection and fellowship, as we recover within the matrix of a caring community of people.

I like the idea of a learning disability, but would add that, different from other learning abilities, addiction is a faulty, crooked, unhealthy, twisted learning experience about who we are, unremembered from a long-ago place we have partially forgotten, but which set the trajectory of our survival.

If uncovered, this negative template of ourselves can be healed. It is called recovery.

Notes or Thoughts

Chapter

How We Learned Attachment

S zalavitz gives us an enormous clue by calling addiction a learning disability. I would go further and deeper by pointing out the great number of addicted folks who learned a faulty position of attachment which led to pain, fear, self-doubt, anger, and anxiety, and then buried that attachment pattern. This pattern was necessary for early survival, but later needs to be uncovered and modified somehow.

The woman who was taken in as an infant, but always remained 'a foster child' because the family refused to legally adopt her. She felt very tentative. Pain.

The guy whose father died when he was ten, leaving him with mother, sister, grandmother, and a brother who bribed him for sexual favors. Confusion.

A man who grew up with drunks for a family, and had to meet a grandfather on the street who was a 'hobo'. Shame.

A young man who had seen his Dad kill his baby sister. Fear and terror.

And the woman who had, as a child, lost several family members 'on a roll'. Grief.

We can see how these early patterns might have happened. No problem.

But the part we MUST see is that they are now buried, and like a thorn covered up with flesh, they must be uncovered somehow, with new and healthy attachment bonds giving us the acceptance and care we need in order to recover.

How does the infant become a person?

At first, Freud's book covers pictured only his lone face.

But as his talking/listening method developed in the hands of others, we notice the psychoanalytic book covers now displaying the Mary Cassatt paintings of the mother and child dyad. Freud's method is recognized as a twosome.

Indeed, the uncountable depictions of the Madonna and babe attest to the fact that something very important takes place in that dyad.

Bowlby might call it affect regulation.

Schore might call it the creation of self-in-relationships.

If it is good enough, people develop healthy ways of relating.

But if the mother or caregiver is depressed, manic, aggressive, brutal...that is another story.

Buried and out of consciousness, a crooked pattern of connection continues to drive a person. This unseen pattern can be so painful that addiction is needed to numb it.

If it is too painful to look at, recovery may be stalled or jettisoned.

Because, we are looking at this painful pattern NOW, but with the eyes and tools of a helpless youngster LONG AGO, who needed to survive above all else, at any cost, which included blocking out the pain of that position needed to survive.

Buried, this pain is 'left behind', but by addiction it can be 'forgotten' and numbed.

And what can uncover this capsule of pain and fear, and heal it?

First, an acceptance that the addicted person is not 'bad', but 'suffering".

Second, an acceptance BY the addicted person that he is not 'bad' but in pain.

Third, seeing that others have become more whole by 'working the steps'.

Fourth, trusting that if others can recover and change, so might I.

Fifth, taking the same actions suggested by the program, slowly but surely.

This is the free, non-coercive path so many have taken, and found recovery.

This framework, this organization has been out there awhile, with amazing results.

This organization is already in place, waiting to be of help. This plan is totally free, and offers the very attachment possibilities that we now know are needed.

So, we can now begin to see HOW the 12Step programs address the twisted, pretzel-like attachment positions that we took on unconsciously long ago, changing them slowly into more comfortable connections with self, others, and the Universe.

Since I have stated that I think for most of us, unconscious old positions of attachment which were too painful to bear led to numbing or substitution by drugs and alcohol, I will try to suggest and illustrate some specific ways that the 12Step framework provides suggested behaviors, attitudes, and relationships to heal.

Working with sponsees has been a wonderful experience for me of new relationship patterns that promote more life-giving health and joy.

We can easily see our pattern of relating as we work with another. Are we too controlling? Are we too laissez-faire? Many things will become evident to us.

And we have our own tools to work on repair.

Notes or Thoughts

Chapter

Coming In to AA

S zalavitz tells of her decision to enter a rehab program, and tells also of her successful 12 Step recovery, which earned her the forgiveness of a 15 year to life sentence for possession of 2.5 kilos of cocaine.

It is evident from her book that she has used her experiences to reach out and help others through writing about addiction. She also writes about the changes needed in that field. She calls for removing shame and stigma.

Coming 'in' is one of the most difficult decisions we make.

We must give up all the ways we avoided the old pain of being uncomfortably attached and muster the courage to admit we have an addiction and are willing to now ask others for help when all we can imagine coming to us is pain or rejection. We must risk the chance that drunks and addicts may be wrong, even though any visits to a 12Step meeting will set us to thinking, because the stories there are proof in themselves of 'something' that brings about life-giving change.

Szalavitz cites the changes very eloquently.

As a child, for whatever reason, she felt unloved and out of kilter for so very many years.

In high school, she finally finds a friend, and this friend introduces her to acid.

Their 'trips' together are wonderful, so attachment and bonding occur through the social connection that is created through drugs.

At Columbia, she gains status and purpose while supplying friends and acquaintances with cocaine, becoming extremely 'popular'.

She is suspended from Columbia for dealing drugs however.

She continues to deal, and is finally busted for possession of 2.5 kilos of cocaine.

Her sentence is 15 years to life.

Both her divorced parents put up their houses to get her out on bail.

It seems to me that at this point she might be said to have been 'hitting bottom'.

'Hitting bottom' is simply a 12Step term for at last beginning to see that you have reached a point of no return.

It is a wake-up call.

It is a turning point.

It is a moment when we find we must contemplate giving up our addicted life.

Right now I am thinking of a current friend whose daughter is addicted to drugs and has been through many rehabs and failed because she MUST have heroin.

This young woman has a two year old daughter that she loves.

Yesterday, child protective services took this dear child away.

The young mom is defiant, blaming each player but herself.

She has so much anger and pain that she needs heroin to simply continue to live.

No one knows at this point how this particular story will end.

My friend is totally helpless to control how this situation will play out.

She has been granted custody of Melody for six months, and at that time the case will be revisited.

Our first reaction is to shame and castigate this young mother for neglecting her little girl.

We could call her a 'druggie' and shake our heads at a person who is 'bad' enough to put her own child at risk.

We could attempt to punish and shame.

Of course 'we' would never do such a thing as give up our child for drugs.

However, do we really know the exact background and experience of another person from conception and birth onward to the present moment?

We can only judge by our own life, which we so often do.

But actually we have no earthly idea what circumstances, large or small, have been endured by another.

And most often the circumstances of another are rooted in mystery.

Let me tell you the story of Robbie.

Notes or Thoughts

Chapter

Robbie

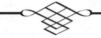

R obbie was in a Kindergarten class of 24 children that I taught in rural Virginia. I still remember a vivid picture he painted while standing at the easel: a bright yellow chick on the green grass below a blue sky.

With young children, any teacher must observe carefully and try to know each young child the best she (or he) can. Young kids are basically forming themselves, and we form ourselves often by how others view us.

Robbie was a real puzzle.

He took books and objects from the lockers of his schoolmates even when reminded over and over about personal property.

Kids and parents grew perturbed.

He would take apart the furniture somehow and the janitor complained.

The office got word of his 'misbehavior', and spoke to me.

At holiday time, we had Kwanzaa, Jewish candles, and my own family Manger Scene, but the baby went missing, despite my 'no touching' instructions.

A couple of days before school closed, I explained to the class that the baby was missing from the crèche, and that I needed it back for my own family Christmas.

On the very last Friday, Robbie arrived and shyly returned the baby to me.

He said, 'I just had to show it to my little sister!'.

Finally, in January, parent-teacher conferences were held and the first couple to sit down with me for a talk were Robbie's parents.

She grew tearful over an unruly boy.

He raised his voice and told me Robbie was BAD. He wanted to punish him and make him be good, and was already spanking him frequently in anger.

So, I made Robbie's house first on my list when I visited each home.

Entering the side door, I noticed a trailer in the drive, very close to the house.

After the visit, Robbie, beaming, followed me through the kitchen to the side door, asking for a cookie as we passed.

His mother said no…it was too near dinner.

But standing in front of the nearby trailer was Robbie's father's mother…with some cookies in her hand.

'Nana has cookies for you, Robbie'.

'I love you best of all!'

Robbie took the cookies and began eating as his mother looked on helplessly.

Here, I felt, was the root of the boy's problem.

I met with the mother later and explained that Robbie was getting mixed messages about rules and boundaries. She had been very emotional about her son's behavior so I knew she might be open for counseling, which she was.

She made an appointment with the local Mental Health Service, and kept it, taking a letter which I had written giving my take, as teacher, on the situation. Finally, Robbie grew calmer and thrived, with behavior now changed for the better, and his troubles subsided to the normal range of any other child in Kindergarten.

The next year, first grade Robbie came back to my room one day after school.

He smiled and explained, 'I just wanted to see where I used to take my nap on the mat in Kindergarten.'

He went to his old spot by the bookcase, paused a moment, then left me with a wave goodbye.

We can see from this vignette that the real root of some problems can lie way back in childhood, totally forgotten and overlooked, or considered inconsequential.

The son who is the spitting image of the husband who fled with another woman.

The homely daughter who is compared constantly to her beautiful sister.

The unseen child who is overshadowed by a needy sibling with disabilities.

The youngster, regardless of their sex, being abused by a close relative.

The child who is hated and ignored by a stepmother.

The list goes on and on.

This person grows up, skewed unconsciously by unhealthy attachment patterns, accepting themselves as bad, ugly, less-than-valuable, stupid, unwanted, helpless.

These feelings can be so intensely painful that the first drink or drug that covers it momentarily can set up the course to addiction.

Maia Szalavitz felt very disconnected as a youngster, but heroin made her feel loved.

Let me say loud and clear that getting at the root of things is really not the place to begin, and it more often may finally remain totally unknown.

But the 12 Steps start a process of delineating and discovering, NOT the root, but first the very tips and tendrils of the outermost twigs and leaves: anger, grief, resentment, low self-esteem, hatred, jealousy, an unforgiving heart.

And this slow discovery process takes place in an atmosphere of total acceptance, where you simply sit in a chair, one among many, and identify your fear and powerlessness out loud, while hopefully working with a sponsor on the Steps.

Notes or Thoughts

Chapter

Each Person
Has a Story

S zalavitz gives a clear description of what, for many of us, starts the whole phase of recovery: a story.

She mentions 'John', whose story resonated with her own, melting her defenses around the edges as she sat in a 12Step meeting.

We are asked to tell our own personal story, a narrative, however long or short, which always has three parts.

What It Was Like
What Happened.
What It Is Like Now.

Like snowflakes, each story is different.

Under the bridge.
Sent to 12 Step treatment.
Now takes meetings to the prisons.

Physician stealing narcotics.
License suspended.
Now recovering in the 12Step rooms, sponsoring others.

The three-part story is always the same, yet totally unique.

Hell-raiser, drinks at work.

She is fired and goes to AA.

Now has three sponsees and a new job.

The stories, and the acceptance, are what enable us to pause, start working with a sponsor on the steps, and slowly begin to allow a new shape to take place in our lives, by way of the tools, and the fellowship.

The stories are also a means of communication.

They are what cause changes in us when all manner of cajoling and persuasion fail.

Often, recovery is not a logical sequence of events taking place in a linear fashion, but a more holistic awakening, with no predictable rhyme or reason, as the old malfunctioning personality position falls away slowly, and bit by bit is replaced by a new, healthier and more authentic self, in tune with others and the Universe.

'It works if you work it' is one of the cardinal slogans in any 12Step program, and the shares in a meeting usually reflect the changes for the better that the members have experienced, or sometimes the pain which is the 'touchstone' of our growth.

We get to know one another, not on a superficial level, but in a deep way as we share from the heart, and that in itself is a profound attachment experience for each one.

Over and over we are reminded that 'love and tolerance is our code'. Not a word needs to be said about the fact that all are accepted, because one look around the room reveals the wide variety of souls that make up the group.

Each one has a different story, yet the theme is always the same: the changes taking place by joining up and using the 'simple kit of spiritual tools'...together.

In some localities, the hour is ended by forming a circle and holding hands.

This is an actual physical manifestation of the unity in the room. We are not just standing there together, but truly 'joining', by clasping the hands of others on either side of us. Joining hands in a circle is a very powerful act, producing body-change.

The larger story seems to be the replacement of a faulty attachment stance formed long ago…by a newer, healthier attachment stance created by the Steps and the fellowship.

We know from her book that Szalavitz went from active addiction to a place of continuing recovery, using her writing skills and experience to help chart a new way of seeing and helping other addicts.

She is clearly an advocate of less punitive attitudes toward the addicted.

Notes or Thoughts

Chapter

Boundaries Versus Punishment

P unishment, shaming, and ridicule have sometimes been used in the addictions field as a misunderstood method for 'bringing people around'. It is tempting to resort to this when we feel frustrated and afraid over the drinking or using done by a friend.

AA has a very basic policy, formulated from the very start, that 'attraction, not promotion' is at the heart of 12 Step program outreach.

Whether we are practicing subtle punishment and shaming, or whether we are preaching and persuading, both of these methods fall short of the suggested way of simple attraction. Personal changes are the best advertisement!

This does not mean we cannot hand an AA pamphlet to someone suffering from an addiction to alcohol.

This does not mean we cannot invite a drunk neighbor to attend an AA meeting.

This does not mean we cannot offer a ride to an addicted teen headed to NA.

What it does mean is that changes in our OWN lives speak far louder than any attempt to trumpet or promote the 12 Step programs.

There is a growing attempt to remove the shame and punitive methods underlying some treatment approaches: name-calling, negative tone-of-voice, insults, punishment. This can push the person further down into his or her addiction.

However, we must continue to hold fast to boundaries.

The Employee Assistance Program offers counseling to those whose jobs are in jeopardy, and the very word 'assistance' speaks of compassion, not judgment.

The breath-alyzer installed in the car of a DUI offender offers a way to keep driving, but with a check on drinking while behind the steering wheel of a vehicle.

Recently I spoke with a doctor after a meeting, and learned that his license had been taken away for five years. Getting it back was contingent on joining AA, getting a sponsor, attending meetings, and working the steps for those five years.

We see from all this that first, boundaries are called to help the addict and those around him.

And second, AA is chosen as the treatment 'suggestion', probably because it is the most widely known and used, with meetings everywhere, at no cost, and showing the most results.

Which is not to say that other programs do not work.

Whatever program works will add to the health of the general population.

But there is no question that the 12 Step program works 'if you work it', and law enforcement will give you that chance.

Just today I am reminded of the fact that the program works.

A young woman I mentioned earlier as having lost custody of her child due to heroin addiction has experienced some changes as of this very day.

Through a series of unexpected events, I am told, she is now in another location, attending meetings, away from her old 'using' friends and actually on a new job!

If she can get sober and clean, showing social services she has given up drugs, she can get her small daughter back in six months.

This is not a case of punishment, but a boundary.

Not a shaming, but the simple fact that her child cannot flourish if her mother continues to use drugs to numb whatever pain she may feel deep inside. The meetings and steps will address that pain; the fellowship is a new 'family'.

Perhaps society needs to take a page from the 12Step programs and make acceptance and faith, along with boundaries, the basic platform of recovery.

The addicts can then accept themselves as valuable, despite wrongs done, and begin to believe that recovery is possible, no matter how farfetched it may seem.

Acceptance is what enables us to pause and see ourselves clearly, no matter what we have done, and not condemn ourselves back into addiction as some kind of punishment we deserve for being so worthless.

This acceptance is palpable in the rooms, if the newcomer can just take hold of it.

Many years ago I worked with depressed twelve year old boys. One had been born of a brutal father and his mother had told him repeatedly each day that he was no good and she wished he were dead. He heard this over and over again.

At the beginning of class we soon instigated a daily ritual of 'taking our vitamins'.

From a large jar with the label VITAMINS, students alternated removing and reading three little strips of paper. These vitamins read:

I am valuable.

I am capable.

I am loved.

We did a skit on Talent Day using this scenario which the audience enjoyed.

Even now, I try to remember these boys, and remind myself that all of us, no matter what we have done...are valuable, capable, and loved.

And boundaries, not condemnations, are necessary.

There is no condemnation in the 12Step literature or in the program itself.

We must take care to remove condemnation as we talk to one another, and as we interact with every newcomer.

Our acts and behaviors and attitudes while drinking or drugging were harmful to ourselves and others, but we can use these to remind those coming in to the program that we, too, were lost in addiction.

But we have changed.

And those changes are called recovery.

Any changes that take place in recovery can be called 'spiritual'.

Notes or Thoughts

Chapter

Implications For Action

In my experience, the slogan 'keep coming back' is one of the most powerful sayings in the 12Step programs because it is an action.

Addiction is made up of many small actions…actually getting one's substance, preparing it, taking it in, hiding it, lying about it, dodging repercussions, etc.

It is only through replacing old actions with new and different actions that we recover.

As a 'grateful recovering alcoholic', I find that the action of coming back to a meeting time after time keeps my recovery green. I hear the joyful experiences of others as they work the steps, and I gain the joy of spiritual growth myself.

We are reminded that it matters not if we WANT to come back.

It is not necessary to wait until we are perfectly delighted to attend a meeting.

Repeated attendance at meetings increases the chance of recovery.

Newcomers are urged to do 'ninety in ninety'.

Ninety meetings in ninety days is a way to replace old habits with new ones.

We repeat this route to the meeting just as we repeated the way to the dealer.

And once in a meeting, we gain a bit of acceptance and serenity which will hopefully grow to replace the frantic numbing of addiction until we need it no more.

But some of the people in the meeting irritate us, and rub us the wrong way!

'Meeting makers make it', is the answer.

Following the tried and true advice to keep coming back, regardless of any feelings of doubt, which surely come, seems to me to be the key to getting a foothold in the recovery program held out by the 12Step approach.

Other programs and ways of recovery may certainly have their successes, but the 12Step way puts a very high priority on connection and acceptance, love and tolerance, thinking of others, and this atmosphere can work wonders.

For those of us who felt less-than, and also those who felt more-than, we begin to become right-sized. Our skewed attachment patterns soften and straighten, and we begin to WANT to attend meetings. This takes time, so we keep coming back.

Someone relapses, and we are filled with doubt and want to quit right away.

But we hear the words 'keep coming back', and perhaps realize that the number of folks clean and sober far outnumber the ones who go back out to addiction.

If we keep at this long enough, we will slowly solidify our new attachment, not to a substance, but now to a group of people who care for us deeply, and who have a set of 'suggestions' for a better life which we can begin to adopt.

Some have an easier time of it than others.

We are cautioned not to judge, but to love them 'until they can love themselves'.

In an atmosphere of acceptance, the pain of what we have done softens, and in working the steps, we are able to recount our 'resentments' and find out more about ourselves and our part, our continuation of old unhealthy patterns.

And the advice to be of service can increase our growing attachment.

Every meeting usually has several 'readings', and as a person begins to take part in this way, the feeling of attachment increases.

Coffee cups may need to be washed, and this involves speaking to those who hand them over to the 'washer', strengthening bonds.

Chairs need to be straightened, spills wiped up, a Kleenex passed to the sharer who becomes emotional.

Here and there, a member may be facing health issues, or financial problems, a divorce, or the death of a loved one, perhaps one who felt the brunt of addiction.

These very personal sharing moments take the recovery ties into a deeper realm, and touch the group profoundly, increasing the strength of attachment and the growing ability to interact with others in a recovery framework.

Notes or Thoughts

Chapter

The Sponsor

The suggestion to get a sponsor is sometimes crucial to recovery.

At first blush it seems insignificant, until we see it in terms of attachment.

In the beginning I could not get a sponsor because I was very isolated and did not really want anyone to know me. I felt a lot of shame.

I tried to study the steps, but without a sponsor I was lost in isolation.

The one thing I did do, however, was continue to attend meetings.

Here I heard over and over how the steps had changed people.

I heard that getting a sponsor was the key.

Finally, I got a sponsor, but never used her.

When members would ask if I had a sponsor, I would answer 'yes'.

But I never once went to that sponsor, and of course she did not do the work and try to persuade me, because you have to WANT recovery enough to reach out and ask.

I was terrified of reaching out.

I simply could not let anyone in.

Finally, I was so miserable and alone that I changed and got another sponsor and began to meet with her, studying the steps, but now with an experienced person I was somewhat ready to open up to.

The sponsor (men with men, women with women) is one who goes over the steps and shares his or her personal experiences of growth.

Rather than a rational, lawyer-like exposition, this sharing touches on emotions, and it is that which can break down the denial which has built up inside the addict.

Meeting together and talking on the phone about specific problems or joys is a huge step in attachment.

We are getting to know someone who has found their way out of addiction.

But more importantly, the care and interest and help of this person begins to pry open the old attachment cage of our own making,

Sponsorship has its dangers, however.

Because recovery is a very difficult undertaking, sponsorship may slowly wind down to just friendship, getting together on a superficial level and skipping the hard slogging of step work.

Getting a sponsor may involve unseen ulterior motivations.

My own sponsor admits openly that in her first choice, she picked someone she felt she could dominate.

Because the 12Step programs counsel self-reflection, she soon realized what she had done and changed to another person.

The general advice of women-to-women and men-to-men addresses the underlying temptation we all have at times to seek out a romantic partner.

Honesty is one cardinal call of 12 Step recovery, and we are constantly called to examine our deepest motives in everything we do.

I finally saw and admitted to myself and others, that I had chosen to have a sponsor in name only, wanting to 'talk the talk' rather than 'walk the walk'.

When I was able to share this fact in a meeting, my honesty could touch others who then might be willing to see where they were putting on a front.

We change in recovery, and it is hard.

To my mind, sponsorship is absolutely essential if we want to change.

We see and hear the changes in others for the better, and this spurs us on to do the things that we are told will bring about change in ourselves.

Not just leaving our old habits and friends and venues.

But doing the things that will bring about changes deep inside.

Speaking to the newcomer.

Leading a meeting.

Putting money in the basket.

Calling another member just to say hi.

Getting up the nerve to ask someone to be our sponsor.

And if that person already has their quota of sponsees, asking another person without giving up and falling back on blame by saying 'it doesn't work'.

Notes or Thoughts

Chapter

29

Helping Sponsees

The AA literature clearly spells out first, the absolute joy of those who first tasted sobriety, and also, the zeal with which they approached other suffering alcoholics with the good news of recovery.

It was agonizingly slow, because at first there were no takers. It was too new.

However, they KNEW it worked, and the doctors, having long given up, saw that it worked, and gladly invited these recovering alcoholics in to talk to drunks admitted to the hospital.

Bill W. and others clearly stated that this work was the very key that kept them sober...trying to help those who were still suffering.

For awhile, I remember thinking that this work had been only practiced by the 'old timers', and was thus no longer necessary since AA has grown exponentially. I was oblivious to the fact that many still practiced helping others, probably because I felt tremendous self-doubt around reaching out and offering a hand, so to speak, myself.

After getting a sponsor myself, I began to understand the power of two women working on the steps together weekly, and staying in touch by telephone.

Still, I was reluctant.

Suppose I did not do it right?

But like a lot of things in the program, I finally made that leap.

I found that the relationship with a sponsee opened my eyes to many things.

First, I was not called to be a friend, or a bank, or a counselor, but simply to be a person who could share my experience, strength, and hope around the steps with another.

One sponsee died drunk, running a red light.

Another told me she wanted to go back to her church to get sober.

A third suffered from Borderline Personality Disorder and needed more help than I was able to give.

So, was I a failure with these sponsees?

Not at all, because I remained sober, and had done my best to share stepwork.

The feeling that I was totally responsible for everything began to drop away.

With the help of MY sponsor, I was learning that I was only responsible for working on the steps with another alcoholic, sharing my experience, and trying to guide them to their own experience with the 12 Steps.

If they were not ready, I was not to blame. They might be ready later.

I began to see how working with another gives us a mirror on our old attachment patterns, and the opportunity to adjust or correct them.

Was I making it too easy?

Was I doing all the work of arranging a time to meet?

Was I afraid to adhere to the power inherent in each step and therefore 'water it down'?

Was I reluctant to admit mistakes I had made myself, wanting to appear more 'recovered' than I really was, to save face?

Was I afraid to raise my hand when the meeting leader asked for those who were willing to be sponsors?

Was I secretly seeking sponsees 'more like me' and not from another cultural background?

The relationship with a sponsee can be a source of great growth and self-knowledge if I am willing to risk.

I have nothing to lose, except more understanding of myself.

Do I want many sponsees as a mark of self-importance? Old outdated pride.

The sponsee is another source of deepening my healthy attachment patterns to myself, to others, and to the Universe and my proper place in it.

Notes or Thoughts

Chapter

The Spiritual Aspect

Controversy swirls around the 'spiritual' aspect of the 12Step programs, and of course there are other ways of getting sober that work.

Many are turned off by any mention of 'God'.

Prayer and thanksgiving can seem quaint and outmoded.

But let's look at things using the framework of attachment.

Early on in 12Step history, the phrase 'as we understood God' was added, and this phrase is the only place in the steps that we see underlined.

This phrase is the key to spirituality in the 12Step programs because it unequivocally takes spirituality out of the domain of formal theology, and places it in the heart of each individual person.

If our initial attachment is tainted with fear, anger, jealousy, grief or lack of normal self-esteem, our view of the Universe is filled with negativity and drinking and drugging becomes necessary to numb out the pain that can result.

Feeling accepted over and over again as we attend meetings in place of our patterns and practices of addiction begins to slowly loosen the power of our old feelings of wrong attachment and the discomfort with our being-in-the-Universe.

Following suggestions, mainly 'keep coming back' allows the heart of the program to slowly touch our own heart, and the stepwork, bit by bit, dismantles our old faulty self, and allows a new self to grow in its place.

Unlike other views of spirituality, this view is extremely down to earth.

If a person is changing, that is spiritual.

If a person is greeting the newcomer, that is spiritual.

If a power-hungry person stoops to wash coffee cups, that is spiritual.

If a sponsor takes a call from a sponsee who has a problem, that is spiritual.

If an isolated person suddenly offers to read The Promises, that is spiritual.

Change is spiritual.

And the 12Step programs are all about change.

All of us fear change.

The literature says we are afraid of becoming the hole in the doughnut.

We shy away from the thought of change, because it is the unknown.

We have lived addicted to our old ways because we know no other way.

But the entire program promotes change.

The speaker who tells of how it was, what happened, and how it is now.

The man or woman who breaks down in tears of joy because now, they can be real now with their children, admitting how the drink or drug took them over.

Reading in the literature the words of Dr. Silkworth, and feeling through his words his pain of seeing alcoholics he could never really help, doomed to die.

Experiencing the wrenching changes as we look at our 'character defects' and understand that there is a Higher Power who can help remove them.

Coming across StepTen's sage truth, 'it is a spiritual axiom that every time we are disturbed, no matter what the cause, there is something wrong WITH US'

Perhaps the word spirituality conjures up old and painful memories of church.

We are advised in this case to use the word 'power', and to look to a higher power, which in the case of AA is usually the group we meet with.

As shares are spoken from around the room, we hear mention of changes that have come to this individual or that one, reminding us that 'it works if you work it'.

If we are into great intellectual propositions and discourses, we may miss the power of the shares.

Too personal.

Too boring.

Too everyday.

Too simple.

But if we listen carefully, we may hear more.

We may discern the slow but sure changing of ordinary people from a place of addiction to a place of growing recovery.

Old and painful attachment patterns are being superseded by new ones.

Sometimes quickly.

Sometimes slowly.

Together, in new attachment relationships we can trust.

Notes or Thoughts

Implications for Prevention

Because addiction is a public health issue, many well-meaning attempts have been made to prevent alcohol or drugs or tobacco from becoming life-threatening. Of course punishment, shaming, and guilt- inducing measures have been used by people who thought this would work. In most cases, it does not.

The 12Step programs put a high priority on accepting the person just exactly where they are, and also encouraging and allowing them to look at themselves honestly.

The current focus on Mindfulness practice in our society seems to be one thing that is helping to create an atmosphere of growth and attitude change.

Jon Kabat-Zinn at the University of Massachusetts Medical School kicked off a tremendous interest in Mindfulness when he instituted the Mindfulness Based Stress Reduction program there and started a very positive trend.

Mindfulness is a difficult thing to 'teach', because most of us are so caught up in the chatter of our minds that we are unable to pause, step back, and simply observe.

Once we get the hang of pausing and observing, we then have tremendous difficulty with the most important part of Mindfulness: throwing out The Judge.

Mindfulness for me is stopping, being in the present moment, and accepting without judgment whatever is going on.

This means noticing with my senses.

The coolness of the breeze.

The smell of the fresh-cut green grass.

The sound of a cricket.

Just being there with it all, and also with my reaction to it, without my critic.

Frequent repetition improves our mindfulness skills.

It can be done anywhere, anytime, by ourselves or with others.

It takes some doing, because we are accustomed to barreling through life, rushing from this to that, with never a moment to 'smell the roses'. It is difficult at first to break the long-held habit of operating on automatic pilot constantly.

Most of us are forever chattering…either out loud or to ourselves.

One man, while dressing to go to work, realized that the committee members he was scheduled to meet with at 9am had been in the shower with him! Instead of feeling the warmth of the water, and the slippery feel of the soap, he had completely left the present moment, and instead jumped ahead to worry and fret about this meeting!

It is difficult to stay in the present moment, but we can learn.

We see the undisciplined nature of our minds and thoughts, and wonder if we can ever learn to simply stop and observe, without judging.

It just takes repeated practice, over and over again.

Even the young can be taught Mindfulness.

I have a book with the tape that goes with it: Sitting Still Like a Frog.

Mindfulness calms the body as we slow down and pause, taking a break from the breakneck speed of today's world, and the ironclad hand of feeling-denial.

And as we leave The Judge aside, we can experience the present moment just as it is, without deciding whether it is good or bad, right or wrong, It just IS.

A certain amount of this mindfulness is incorporated into the 12Step programs.

We put down the drink or drug, and then we observe and contemplate life with no judgment, only noticing how it feels to lay aside addiction.

As we work through the Steps, with a sponsor and the meetings holding us close, we can then work on seeing our resentments, our faulty patterns, our hurtful ways with others, and then with the 'kit of spiritual tools' learn to practice other patterns.

Perhaps we cannot find ourselves on the mountaintop of purity, but down in the messy journey through our fears, resentments, frailties, grief, anger, and worry. We must banish The Judge, and experience ALL feelings just as they are, without exception.

Helping others to do this, especially kids, can be a joyful thing.

Preventing addiction starts early, by allowing human beings to awaken to the moment.

Addiction is an unthinking occupation, trying to reach the numbness that cuts us off from ourselves, others, and the Universe with our unique place in it.

Making a place for Mindfulness in our schools, where youngsters first experiment with drugs and alcohol to be 'cool' and impress peers, would be an enormous step in the 'war on addiction'.

It is difficult to see the connection, especially if you are not addicted, but there is a huge connection between practicing mindfulness and breaking through denial.

Solitary meditation can have its focus on a mantra, a state, a feeling, a virtue, a higher place. For me, somehow this led to more isolation, and less in-sight.

But Mindfulness includes EVERYTHING as we go about our day and become aware of the messy mix of feelings and states, pains and frustrations, sounds, sights, smells, and textures. We can experience ourselves as part of the great tapestry of being, and perhaps in this way circumvent the power of drugs and alcohol to numb us out.

Notes or Thoughts

Chapter

Learning to Talk
and Listen

If we go back to the first paradigm, neuroscience tells us it is the mother, or caregiver, in relation to the child, who provides the very first affect regulation experiences. It is this that begins the development of a 'self'.

For addiction prevention, it might be necessary to change the zeitgeist, by education and relentless reminders, from the current focus on just teens, to a wider focus on the development of the person from conception onward. It is the events early on which mold us into who we are, and what we feel about ourselves. It is the earlier attachment pattern, faulty or not, which is important to address.

The ACE study tells us of the high correlation between adverse childhood experiences and addiction.

This points us to more parent education, more pregnancy support, and even other measures.

Colorado has made birth control free and available, reducing by a large margin the incidence of abortion and unwanted pregnancies.

Teens could be counseled more deeply to understand unhealthy motivations for sex, like wanting to be popular, for instance.

There needs to be a shift, from emphasis on academic progress alone, to the inclusion of feelings.

Daniel Goleman, in his book Emotional Intelligence makes the case that social and emotional learning can sometimes matter more than IQ, or our intelligence score.

In the rooms, these old and painful attachment patterns are healed by the talking and listening that goes on.

A member raises a hand to share, and is therefore granted an opportunity to talk about a current problem or victory.

This place to 'talk' can heal old emotional wounds where one was not allowed to talk, or forbidden to talk, thus driving feelings down so deep they could not be readily accessed.

We all know the extremely 'smart' person who is intellectually advanced, but has no notion at all about feelings, whether their own, or that of another.

Sometimes our deepest feelings of inferiority, or even grandiosity, can stem from long ago patterns built in at an early age.

These feelings remain, unexcavated, only to emerge so strongly that we turn to addiction to numb them out.

It is the fortunate person who can end up in AA, with an experienced sponsor, and a group of recovery-oriented fellow-travellers, sharing on Steps 6 and 7 while others listen intently.

It is difficult to talk about these strong feelings, because often they come with the intensity of the original situation when small and vulnerable.

But as we get it out, we gaining recovery, not only from addiction, but the bondage of old personality patterns instituted in the iron-clad days of our childhood.

As we recover, these old feelings can pop out unexpectedly, surprising us and others by their power. This means we are healing and changing for the better.

Notes or Thoughts

Chapter

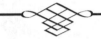

Dan Siegel

D an Siegel is an 'internationally acclaimed author, award winning educator, and renowned child psychiatrist'. These are the words from the internet and YouTube.

I first came across this man by listening to his DVD on the interpersonal neurobiology of the WE, and have followed him ever since.

He is probably one of the most far-thinking persons of our day, and his book, The Whole-Brain child is about the developing minds of children, and how we, as parents, can interact with them to foster maximum mind development.

Most of our emphasis in the past has been on how to improve ourselves as adults. But Siegel's focus here begins with our earliest interactions with our children, an area we are inclined to ignore.

Many people think of babyhood as a time to take cute pictures of the adorable child and how he or she looks, only to forget that a 'self' is rapidly forming, for better or for worse.

The good news is that a dawning recognition of the importance of early development is taking place.

Siegel gives parents information about the brain, but adds the revolutionary step of outlining specific ways to interact with their child to put in place positive ways of living, with an emphasis on the give and take of human relationships.

Rather than seeing childhood as simply a period of waiting until school-learning can take place, Siegel makes the case, with his brilliant backdrop descriptions of brain activity, for a new view of the early life of a child as the place and time to create emotional health which will last a lifetime.

With this approach, we can see a definite change from the view we have so often had in the past.

Rather than putting all our time, effort, and money into programs for school-age kids and teens, we can have that 'aha' moment, by reading this book, that more emphasis should be placed on the earliest interactions in the life of a child. Siegel is helping parents see new ways to foster self-confidence and compassion early on, which will last, hopefully, through the later years when depression, doubt, and old negative feelings might play into the power of drugs and alcohol to momentarily help forget emotional pain.

For now, the 12Step programs offer a way and a place to examine those old faulty configurations of how things do not work, and how to slowly change that.

The middle steps instruct us to look at our resentments, our 'character defects', and how our old patterns hurt others.

We do this, not in an atmosphere of punishment, but with accepting people who have looked at their own faulty patterns, and who show us new ways of being, while reminding us that change is about 'progress, not perfection'.

We are not responsible for the ways we grew early in life into negative positions, but we ARE responsible for observing those positions, and for accepting help which can slowly change them.

Otherwise we remain stuck, miserable, angry, fearful, full of self-doubt.

And our relationships reflect our negative stance.

Siegel is doing us an enormous favor, by shifting the examination of patterns of relationship from grade-school and college, way back to the very first years.

For the past week or so, I had noticed Aaron missing at the regular noon meeting.

Asking around, I learned that he was back in rehab, and that his sponsor had only been informed by his wife.

Knowing Aaron, and parts of his story, I was not surprised.

He carried great burdens from a childhood with a mother who was emotionally sick, for whatever reason, herself.

His growing up years, he told me, were lived in a milieu of alcohol, drugs, and prostitution.

No wonder he could not learn to read. His brain was dealing with pain and confusion. He was probably branded as 'bad'.

The most searing incident I heard from him was when he went to his mother in desperation and begged her to help him learn to read so he would not be demoted to a section of much younger kids.

Her reply, 'I don't give a fuck if you never learn to read'.

I hesitate to put into words what Aaron's attachment must have felt like, and how deep his feelings of inadequacy must be.

The good news is that in the 12Step programs he can come back to a room full of people who love him, and accept him, and cheer him on if he chooses.

I will be there to give him a hug if I continue to work my own recovery program.

Notes or Thoughts

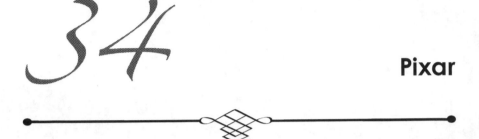

Chapter

34

Pixar

P ixar is making films that clarify and validate feelings to children, and Inside Out is a perfect example of a growing trend to educate kids about their feelings and better ways to understand and handle them. This is basic and crucial childhood education.

Inside Out features a young girl, Riley, who has to move with her family to a distant and unfamiliar location.

The movie features five characters to introduce five common feelings that we all experience from time to time. Dr. David Schwartz has infused Internal Family Systems theory into this powerful and delightful film.

The importance of identifying feelings harks all the way back to Charles Darwin, who found that certain affect states were common to all cultures, fundamental parts of being human, necessary for survival and basic everyday living.

I won't reveal the story line of the movie and spoil it for you, but I will address the five emotional characters, perfectly done in both outfit and facial expression, not to mention splendid voice-overs. I bought all five dolls from Hallmark to use with kids.

My very favorite is anger.

Anger is a bright-hot red man with proper tie and dress shirt, eyes glaring, and mouth frozen in an angry grimace. I like him because anger is one of the most powerful emotions, and one often displayed by children in day-to-day interactions.

It is also a feeling that we have trouble dealing with, understanding, and controlling.

Fear is a pale purple guy, scared into a frozen state of paralysis by whatever he is so terribly afraid of. His hair is literally standing on end due to fright, and he sports a hound's tooth vest and pink tie. His eyes are crossed, stuck in a state of pure unadulterated fear.

Disgust (Darwin postulated that this emotion grew out of the smell of rotting food) is all dressed up in a green dress with a pink scarf at her neck. Her expression is truly one of disgust, with eyes and mouth curling in contempt, clearly conveying the feeling that whatever-it-is must be placed out of bounds, beyond the pale.

For sadness, the colors of course are blue. One shade of aqua blue for face and hands, and a darker blue for hair and body. She definitely has 'the blues', with mouth turned down, and eyes behind her glasses pleading with us to notice and be sympathetic to her depressed state.

Finally, joy is the fifth feeling. This doll was sold out of every store I went to, and had to be bought online at a hefty price. Maybe parents felt more comfortable with joy.

She has a perky hairdo, a great little smile, and guileless eyes, wide open, plus a yellow dress dotted with small flowers.

Inside Out is a tour de force, with a gripping story, plenty of entertaining sequences and sidelines, and a very healthy educational focus on feelings.

Children and adults both can learn from this movie, and improve familiarity with the important role that emotions play in our lives.

It seems that this theory of Internal Family Systems was very influential in the creation of Inside Out. This is a theory that has a proven track record.

If so, perhaps those who view it will have less need for this kind of therapy as they grow up, making friends with and understanding all emotional states.

And not just JOY.

All of our emotions protect and guide us.

All of our emotions can keep us from harm.

Our emotions are valid, even sadness, which can underscore things and people we love and miss when they are gone.

Pixar is doing a great job in preventing addiction, because so much about addiction is basically to cover up painful old emotional states, buried but still alive.

Notes or Thoughts

Chapter

Oxytocin

Mother Nature has provided our bodies with a hormone, Oxytocin, which is associated with attachment and bonding.

When is the last time you hugged someone, or shook hands, or gazed with real connection at a friend while they were talking?

When is the last time you had a small dog or cat lovingly in your arms?

All these are signs that we are mammals, whose brains are set up for, and rewarded for, connection.

Oxytocin is produced in the hypothalamus and then secreted into the bloodstream, with rewarding feelings of attachment and well-being. Love, if you will.

Nature provides Oxytocin bountifully at important times like childbirth and breast feeding to ensure the bonding between a mother and her offspring.

Oxytocin floods the participants at the time of orgasm, making sure the species will survive and continue to propagate.

It is said that Oxytocin can promote healing.

In the moving book, Possibilities, by N. Turner Simkins, we are given a story that exemplifies the power of attachment and family bonding, and possibly the healing effects of Oxytocin on the physical body.

Tara and Turner have three sons. Their middle son, Brennan, was struck with leukemia at a very early age, as a first grader.

The book takes us along with this family through four bone-marrow transplants and many stays at St. Jude Hospital in Memphis before a final return to 'normal' life.

There are numerous times that Brennan's very life was at stake.

What impresses the reader is the attachment and deep devotion of the Turner family as they lovingly support Brennan and determine to do everything possible for his well-being.

At times, the entire family moves lock, stock, and barrel to Memphis, with the two brothers even attending school there.

After the third failed bone-marrow transplant, things are looking extremely grim since a fourth transplant had never been done before at St. Jude.

Brennan's mother, Tara, steps up to donate her cells for what might be a last try.

Somehow, miraculously, this procedure does work, and ultimately Brennan finally is allowed to return home, and the family resumes its everyday paces, with a few modifications.

What is so significant about this story is the clear message that the attachment to Brennan was unequivocal.

This is a far cry from the historical view that children 'won't remember'.

Indeed, children do remember, somewhere deep down in their cells.

From the determined attachment and connection of the family to Brennan, and the physical presence of them as a loving and caring nearby 'caress', there probably was some Oxytocin produced.

This family is an outstanding example of how attachment, bonding, and connection can benefit all who partake.

And a reminder that we are created, as mammals, to love and care for one another.

I have never spoken to anyone at St. Jude.

But my guess is that they put a high premium on supporting the closeness of families when they treat a youngster because they know it helps

We cannot count on this working every single time for ultimate healing.

But we can all be thankful that Brennan was granted life.

I am convinced Oxytocin was involved somehow!

Supporting and caring for others becomes an everyday occurrence in the 12Step programs because we truly care that others get clean and sober. We know how our lives have changed and want that change for those who join up with us.

While I was writing this book, a new guy, Willie, raised his hand as a newcomer.

After the meeting, I shook his hand and found out he had been sent by Freedom House, and that he just wanted to find out about more about AA.

He came to the Noon meeting every day, and I would chat with him over the coffee pot. We are told to support others because it takes us out of self, and for those few minutes I forgot the stress of writing because I was truly interested in him.

Days passed, and finally Willie shared he had been having blackouts from alcohol.

Finally, on a Thursday, Willie answered the white chip offer at the end of the meeting, and actually joined up with the 12Step program, becoming part of us.

The joy of this event loosened my writer's block, and the next chapter began to flow.

I attribute this to the Oxytocin produced by getting out of 'self', caring for another.

Notes or Thoughts

Chapter

Oxycontin

I was at wit's end about this chapter until I led an AA meeting this morning at 7am.

The Daily Reflections book fell open to March 2nd…a far cry from the actual date.

The topic was 'Hope', and the line that hit me was 'May I always remember that the power within me is far greater than any fear before me'.

Expecting a wooden reception, I nevertheless shared about the hormone Oxytocin, and my feeling that it connected with the emphasis on 'WE' in the 12Step programs.

I shrank with discouragement, and felt embarrassed as I recited Wikipedia's description of Oxytocin's power around childbirth and orgasm, and its presence when we shake hands, hug, or even attend carefully to another.

My coffee cup was empty, until Tyrone motioned that he would get me more. When he returned with my steaming brew, I felt that surge of togetherness. The room was full of people, and folks were sharing on the topic of hope…one an out-of-town visitor.

I mentioned that it was difficult not to say Oxycontin for Oxytocin, because that substance is well known in recovery circles, and rolls off the tongue with familiarity.

Each time I mentioned Oxytocin, I had to pause to recall this unfamiliar word, and pronounce it slowly and correctly.

Shares began to come easily and frequently from this group, for we all knew that addiction was isolating, and recovery was about connection.

Finally, Michael wrapped up the meeting, after a lot of thought, by commenting that our meeting and sharing and hugging and caring for one another WAS our new Oxycontin, giving us what we were really seeking in our addiction. That feeling is what I call attachment. Attachment to caring others mends the isolation that we felt in addiction, and restores our connection to ourselves, others, and the Universe.

After the meeting, I overheard a beautiful blonde newcomer tearfully confessing her unbreakable addiction to Oxys to a friend. We all exchanged telephone numbers.

Patrick Kennedy, in A Common Struggle, gives us a very personal account of his break with the denial of a very public and proud political family whose weaknesses needed always to be hidden.

His pain as a child of a second-generation alcoholic mother jumps out of the pages.

His pain as a child of a father who lost three brothers, two to gruesome assassinations played endlessly on the television screen.

His own pain in keeping this enormous family pain down with the help of addiction.

Patrick is very vocal about the changes that the 12Step fellowship brought about for him, and is now using his famous name to modify mental health legislation, since addiction IS a grave mental health problem.

Tommy Rosen is another whose life changes spurred him on to create and establish Recovery 2.0.

Many are now seeing the connection between addiction and earlier childhood patterns often begun in the family that can be changed, like Dan Siegel.

It is my hope that this book may set someone, maybe you, to be thinking and rethinking the myriad causes of addiction.

Setting firm boundaries around the results of drinking and drugging are needed, but shame and stigma are not.

May we, together, find much earlier causes of addiction, and address them.

May we support programs like AMIkids, which seeks out those children who are struggling, and gives help.

May we encourage more documentation of very early events following birth.

May we promote social and emotional learning, following the example of Daniel Goldman.

I will close with a memory about Frances, a four year old. She was adopted, and a sunny, delightful little girl she was. But…

One day she came into school and threw the crayons against the wall. She bit another child, and refused to join us at circle time.

A call to her mother revealed a report of nothing different. No job changes. No grandmother visiting. No house redecorations.

Stumped, we were about to end the conversation when Frances's Mom said she had a secret to tell me.

I asked what it was.

WE ARE PREGNANT. With our own baby! Bob brought me a dozen roses last night!

Children are extremely perceptive, and I urged her to break this news to Frances as soon as she could.

The next week Frances was calm and happy, sharing the family news at Circle.

We must put more emphasis on helping the child and the family much, much earlier.

And if we do, we can foster more Oxytocin.

And people will need less Oxycontiin.

Notes or Thoughts

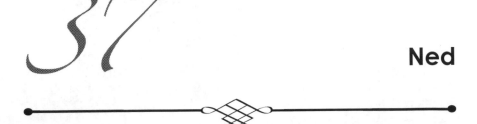

Chapter

37

Ned

Just now, after texting AA Yvonne to drive safely, and getting a great reply, I thought of Ned.

Ned is a big burly muscular guy that was prone to mano a mano fights when he was drinking. He was a hell raiser, and drank continually to 'get drunk and pass out'. He almost always sat next to me at the Noon meeting, sharing with his Jersey accent.

He was prone to be a prankster, and would often hide my purple umbrella until I got mad and told him to quit. (Part of recovery is learning to set boundaries.)

When I asked him to listen to my first chapter for errors, he promptly agreed, later confessing that he was honored.

We met over coffee and sat at a secluded table for privacy.

He told me more of his story, but what stood out was his account of being called as a volunteer right after 9.11.

Iron workers and steel workers were among the first volunteers dispatched to search the wreckage, so he qualified…a union man.

As he began to speak, he pulled out his handkerchief and wiped his eyes. As he told about the overpowering smell, the 'stink' of death and destruction they worked in, the tears flowed. He said a priest had been sent to minister to the volunteers as they worked at their indescribable task.

At one point, the priest advised Ned that he was showing signs of PTSD. Ned could not stop himself. If he could help save just one barely surviving person!

Earlier in our conversation, without any emotion, but with a rueful snort, Ned had described his childhood as the oldest.

He said as soon as his father got home from work, the brutal beating would begin, as an example to the younger kids.

Over and over he was beaten by his father, and this continued day after day until he was old enough and big enough to be let alone.

Ned continued to live out this script...beat or be beaten.

Now, in recovery, he has tremendous remorse for his actions.

He shares in order to reach the newcomer who might be looking back on his own brutality.

But I could not help wondering if part of his 9.11 grief could not have been the unspoken, 'buried under cement' grief of a boy completely overcome physically by a father determined to beat the living daylights out of his son, frequently and unmercifully.

The child 'forgets' because attachment is necessary for survival to the young.

What about Diane?

Each year, when summer begins to simmer down, and the first cool breeze of fall touches our face, Diane is reminded of this memory from childhood.

It was on such a day in the coolness of early fall, that Diane and her brothers were out in the back yard playing with their four dogs.

These dogs were more like siblings, and the children got a lot of their love and connection needs met in a troubled family by romping and cuddling with these pets.

The kids were making a lot of noise, and Dad was drunk and very touchy.

Suddenly he grabbed his rifle from the truck and then began to aim carefully.

One by one, he killed the four dogs, as his kids looked on in frozen horror, hearing the loud shots and seeing the blood.

The screen door slammed as Dad left the scene and entered the kitchen, gun still in hand.

Why was Diane unable to let this memory go?

Because her attachment and survival depended on storing this warning, but her ongoing day to day functioning demanded that 'forget'.

It was only in the secure recovery rooms that Diane, who drank to cover depression, was able to start healing.

Notes or Thoughts

Chapter

Vincent Fellite MD and
12 Step Recovery

I f there were only one wish I could have granted, it would be for everyone to view and understand the interview that I saw with Vincent Fellite.

It was back in the 80's that Kaiser Permanente was doing a study of obesity, which was obviously a health issue.

A night nurse in a retirement facility who weighed 408 pounds was instructed to lose weight, but she could not. She gained it back quickly if at all successful.

After the bariatric surgery, she STILL gained it back!

Crazy behavior? Hard headed woman? Impossible case?

Turns out she had been repeatedly molested by a grandfather when young. He would wake up at night and come to her bed in the dark.

The huge addition of flesh was her WALL against things she could not speak of.

The job served two functions...being sure oldsters were sleeping, and also unconsciously allowing herself to sleep during daylight hours!

The obesity study was so revealing about early trauma and how to 'listen' to it that Kaiser Permanente decided to include in their general health questionnaire a few questions about childhood traumatic episodes...against the strong objection of some who felt that these negative experiences should not be mentioned or stirred up.

These questions were left sprinkled into the health questionnaire and this had rather astounding results.

The examining physician had an entry into 'adverse childhood experiences' and were also told to probe the question about how the patient then dealt with this.

SOMEONE WAS LISTENING!

This health study included thousands, and the Centers for Disease Control began to take notice.

The correlation between the traumatic childhood experiences and addictions was mind-boggling.

Over-eating, sex, alcohol, drugs, nicotine (one guy who discovered his hanged father when young ended up smoking 7 packs a day), and crystal meth (used in the first anti–depressants) all seemed to provide a chemical antidote to 'brain stress'.

Being able to verbalize anxiety (Balint) at last gave some soupcon of relief.

As the analyst Alice Miller termed it, 'enlightened witnessing' proved healing.

The number of office visits to see the doctor, with just this simple question and answer survey, was reduced by 35%!

These are often unspeakable experiences.

Finally opening up to someone who is willing to hear perhaps provides enough oxytocin or other chemicals to manage the pain of remembering.

A Vietnam vet who asked a buddy to cover for him briefly later found the familiar body strung up on a rope between two trees.

The entire body had been skinned.

I, myself, have a hard time just breathing when I write those words.

It is my understanding that many, if not most, in all of the 12 Step programs cover up pain with some kind of addictive substance or behavior.

The Steps first uncover the negative results of that addiction.

But as we dig deeper, in Steps 4,5,6,7,8 and 9 we peel back our more obvious patterns, and find underneath the gold of an original 'me' that is totally accepted in the 'rooms', imperfect but able to tolerate the intolerable.

It is with the personal sponsor that we can regain better relational skills.

It is in the circle of a meeting that we can admit that we drank, stole, or lied.

And gradually, as in peeling back the layers of an onion, we accept the oxytocin or whatever healing chemicals there might be in the room, from a band of brothers.

Or, we go back to the Oxycontin of our choice to numb out.

Please read the book Tribe by Sebastian Junger.

He speaks of the chemistry underneath the togetherness of the 12 Step programs in my estimation.

'When a person does something for another person–a prosocial act, as it's called–they are rewarded not only by group approval but also by an increase of dopamine and other pleasurable hormones in their blood. Group cooperation triggers higher levels of OXYTOCIN (caps mine),for example, which promotes everything from breast-feeding in women to higher levels of trust and group bonding in men. Both reactions impart a powerful sensation of well-being. Oxytocin creates a feedback loop of good –feeling and group loyalty that ultimately leads members to "self-sacrifice to promote group welfare" in the words of one study.'

People who relapse often come back and say that they drifted away from the 12 Step meetings, or their sponsor, or their sponsees. Perhaps they drifted away from the powerful Oxytocin of the fellowship back to the power of Oxycontin…addiction.

We may be discovering how togetherness heals, and more importantly, how early togetherness inoculates.

One day at a time.

One moment at a time.

In tune with the Universe.

Now.

Notes or Thoughts

Chapter

Leroy

Yesterday Leroy called and asked me to give my story at Sunday's meeting. None of us accepts speaking to a group without some trepidation.

But I overcome all doubts and fears at the sound of Leroy's voice.

He and have a strong connection in the AA program....oxytocin kicks in.

Each person's story is an account of change and recovery...oxytocin kicks in.

I am familiar with the meeting's locale which is at a treatment center. There will be people who have 'hit bottom' and also many more people who have found that the 12 Step program works and gives us a new life...oxytocin kicks in.

I will use a visual aid.

On a poster board I have made a chart.

It is a chart of the pattern of life for us recovering addicts

Ages 0 to 17 is a red line.

These are the formative years.

Ages 17 to 56 is a black line.

These were my dark years.

Ages 56 to 81 is a green line.

These years are green because these are my truly living years, recovering life and sharing and exchanging life with others in the fellowship.

One moment at a time.

Notes or Thoughts

The Family Photo

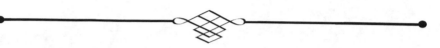

This photo is one of my extended family. I am to the left with my two little boys very close to me.

They gave me bountiful Oxytocin with their presence, enough to see me through…

Notes or Thoughts